CAKES FOR KIDS

Sarah Stacey

Photographs by Chris Ridley

· ELM TREE BOOKS · LONDON ·

BEFORE YOU BEGIN

Read the recipe through carefully before you start

Times given are a rough guide to *decorating*. Obviously it may take you a bit longer the first time. You can usually do a lot of the cake the day before to relieve pressure on the day of the party. Allow extra time for baking cakes and making icing if you are going to do this yourself

If you are in any doubt, read the section on basic cake-making and icing (p. 7–15) first. Remember that fan ovens take less time than conventional ovens

Don't worry if you can't find exactly the sweet or colouring I've used. Anything similar will do

Don't leave cakes decorated with chocolate in a warm place

First published in Great Britain 1986
by Elm Tree Books/Hamish Hamilton Ltd
Garden House, 57–59 Long Acre, London WC2E 9JZ

Copyright © 1986 by Sarah Stacey

Book design by David Warner
Drawings by Patrick Leeson

British Library Cataloguing in Publication Data
Stacey, Sarah
    Cakes for kids.
    1. Cake decorating
    I. Title
    641.8'653   TX771
    ISBN 0-241-11793-3

Typeset by Rowland Phototypesetting Ltd
Bury St Edmunds, Suffolk
Printed and bound in Spain
by Cayfosa Industria Gráfica, Barcelona
Dep. Leg.: B.13330-1986

CONTENTS

INTRODUCTION

I have a hazy happy memory of decorating a birthday sponge cake for my brother. I think I was about twelve at the time. I can remember beating things endlessly with a wooden spoon and then decorating the cake with butter cream icing – not quite enough to cover the top – glacé cherries and bits of angelica. Much later, as a so-called 'professional' cook, I went on to make all sorts of dishes for all sorts of people, but from that sponge cake until last year when Elm Tree Books asked me to suggest some ideas for children's party cakes, my cake decorating career stood still.

The idea of making and decorating cakes for children was so attractive that I decided to have a go. I made the tryout cakes in Singapore, where I happened to be at the time. The climate was a nightmare – the icing ran faster than I could – and so was the lack of a proper kitchen. There was a gas hob but no oven, so I bought the actual cakes, then cut them up and decorated them with pounds of homemade icing, using only a plastic saucepan, an ordinary table knife, spoon and teaspoon and an awfully large chopping cleaver which went with the resident wok. Feeling intrepid but insecure, I started off with Paddington Bear. To my astonishment, he turned out to be easy to make and endearing to look at and, what was more, he was very much like the original. I was excited and pleased – maybe this book would work after all.

At first, I wasn't sure how to approach the book. Because I had little experience with cakes apart from eating them, and no formal training as a cook, it obviously couldn't be a superior manual about complicated cake-making, and I was uncertain how much time and knowledge most mothers would bring to the task of decorating cakes. So I talked to as many parents as I could and the way this book is written is the result of their suggestions.

Most of them loved the idea of making exciting and original cakes for their child's party but didn't have much time to devote to it. And, as one of them said to me ruefully, 'I only make a cake twice a year but when I do, it's supposed to be brilliant.'

I hope this book makes it clear that producing wonderful cakes can be fun and fast, and is much more a matter of assembling ready-made items in the right order than of being a brilliant cake-maker. After all, you can buy the cake from a local shop if you want to – or use a cake-mix.

I talked to the children too, as much as to their parents, and I went to their parties. Having a better cake than your friend whose party was last week is very important. A Computer cake, for instance, was much more exciting than your age in a number cake. I learnt something else too. A piece of sponge cake is pretty boring in itself, just like any other day's cake; it is the bits you can pick off which count: the Smarties, the Chocolate Buttons, the Flakes and Dolly Mixtures. My Erupting Volcano cake (page 20) is surrounded by pounds of chocolate rubble and rock. Within minutes of that particular cake being set on the table, I saw fourteen seven-year-olds completely clear the rubble and the rocky outcrop, leaving only the chocolate volcano cake – for their parents to eat up!

I came across a few problems both with making and icing these cakes, and sometimes they were the sort that make you feel like throwing the whole lot away, so there is a section at the end of the book called Disasters (p.127). You can salvage almost anything and this chapter tells you how.

I also want to point out that it is possible to decorate every one of these cakes without having to pipe the smallest squiggle. People who are expert at piping will see where they can have fun; for those like me who are not keen, it isn't necessary.

Once I decided how to do it, I had a wonderful time planning and writing this book. Most of the cakes were made for real children and first appeared at their parties. I found it was much more fun making cakes for children I knew and could watch devouring them, rather than just carrying out a design. I was endlessly delighted at the children's excitement when they saw their cakes and I collected some marvellous thank you letters and some very sticky kisses.

I hope you enjoy making these cakes as much as I have.

ACKNOWLEDGMENTS

I would like to thank the following grown-ups:

Jackie Clarke, Gillian Greenwood, Ian Hanson, Tessa Hayward, Bryan Kemp, Jenny Reuvid, Chris Ridley, Clive Syddall, Caroline Taggart, Adrian Webster;

and the following children:

Nimrata Budrani, Katie Campbell, Georgina Campbell, Jessica Cran, Polly Drew, Rory Edgerton, Benjamin Georget, Carl Johannes Hamilton, Jamie Jones, Andrew MacDonald, Kate Pakenham, Tom Pakenham, Alexandra Sandell, Thomas ap Simon, Nicholas ap Simon, Jessica Stansfeld, Max Webster.

USEFUL ADDRESSES

The following companies stock a wide range of kitchen equipment, ingredients and decorations, and were very helpful to me while I was writing this book. They all operate mail-order services.

Graham and Green, 4 & 7 Elgin Crescent, London W11. 01-727 4594 (for accessories)

Divertimenti, 68–72 Marylebone Lane, London W1. 01-935 0689; 139-141 Fulham Road, London SW3. 01-581 8065

Covent Garden Kitchen Supplies, 46 Bourne St, London SW1. 01-730 3123

David Mellor, 4 Sloane Square, London SW1. 01-730 4259; 26 James St, London WC2. 01-379 6947; 66 King St, Manchester 2. 061-834 7203

BASICS

EQUIPMENT
FOR MAKING CAKES:
Measuring scales; Food processor or Food
Mixer or Pudding basins, wooden and
metal spoons; Cake tins, well greased,
floured and lined with Bakewell paper;
Rubber spatula; Palette knife (optional)

FOR WRAPPING CAKES:
Clingfilm

FOR MEASURING CAKES:
Ruler and tape measure

FOR CUTTING UP CAKES:
Large knife with serrated edge; Small
sharp knife

TO ICE CAKE ON:
Upturned pudding basin, dinner or soup
plate or icing turntable

FOR MAKING ICING:
Measuring scales; Nylon sieve; Pudding
basins; Wooden spoons

FOR ROLLING OUT ICING:
Large pastry board; Rolling pin; Flour
dredger filled with ½/½ cornflour and icing
sugar; Bakewell paper

FOR SIEVING AND SPREADING APRICOT
JAM:
Small saucepan; Wooden spoon; Sieve;
Pastry brush

FOR PAINTING CAKES:
Small paint brushes, in about 3 sizes

FOR MIXING COLOURS:
Jam-jar tops

FOR PUTTING ON SMALL DECORATIONS:
Eyebrow tweezers

FOR ALL SORTS OF THINGS:
Scissors, glue, sellotape, cocktail sticks,
cake boards, wrapping paper, pencils

INGREDIENTS AND DECORATIONS
CAKES:
Soft margarine (or butter); Caster sugar;
Self raising flour; Size 2 eggs; Baking
powder; Powdered chocolate; Oranges or
lemons

FONDANT:
Icing sugar; Liquid glucose; Size 2 eggs

MARZIPAN:
Ground almonds; Size 2 eggs; Icing and
caster sugar; Vanilla; Rose or Orange
Flower Water (optional)

BUTTER CREAM:
Soft margarine or unsalted butter; Icing
sugar; Flavouring

ROYAL:
Icing sugar; Lemon juice; Size 2 eggs;
Glycerine

CHOCOLATE YOGHOURT:
Greek yoghourt or sour cream; Plain block
chocolate

GLACÉ:
Icing sugar

DREDGING MIXTURE:
Cornflour; Icing sugar

CAKE GLUE:
Apricot jam (cheapest)

CAKE FILLINGS:
Butter cream icing; Lemon curd; Jam

COLOURINGS:
Cake colouring liquids (from supermarkets
and stores); Concentrated cake colouring
pastes (from specialist cook shops); Edible
gold and silver powder (from specialist
cook shops); Non-toxic gold and silver
paint (from art shops and stationers)

DECORATIONS:
Hundreds and Thousands; Silver and
coloured balls; Angelica; Small sweets
from supermarkets and corner shops; Cake
candles and holders

CAKE-MAKING

These notes are for inexperienced cake-makers, as I was when I started writing this book! For most of the party cake recipes, you can buy ready-made cakes of approximately the right size. If necessary, trim ones which are much too large, or put two or more together to build up a big cake. Alternatively you could use a cake mix and bake the mixture in an appropriate sized tin. Check on the size of cake the packet will make and double up on the quantity if necessary.

Deciding on a recipe

I have used Victoria and Madeira sponges for the cakes in this book. I tried making them by three different methods: by hand, which made the lightest and best risen cakes but took the longest; by food mixer, which made the next lightest and took rather less time; and by food processor, which was by far the quickest but produced marginally less well-risen cakes. All three methods, however, produced delicious cakes using these recipes. I tested the recipes time and again, and both quantities and oven temperatures are as accurate as I can make them.

Points to Note

Victoria sponges behave predictably used in 3 and 4 egg mixtures, either for sandwich or single tin cakes. 5 or 6 egg mixtures can sink in the middle, so for these I use Madeira cakes.

Food processor Madeira cakes will not stand upright for any length of time – so do check before you start whether this is going to be necessary.

I used soft margarine for all the cakes in this book. The difference in taste between margarine and butter is slight, especially to children, and it is much cheaper and easier to cream. You can, if you prefer, use butter in any of these recipes, as long as it is very soft.

Preparation

Decide which recipe you will use and read it carefully. Please also read through the following points; they will save you time and bother.

Cold ingredients may curdle cakes; at least one hour before making the cake, stand all ingredients at room temperature, measure out the margarine (or butter) and spread it on a plate in a warm place.

At least twenty minutes before you plan to put the cake in the oven, make certain that the shelf is in the middle, light the oven and set it to the correct temperature.

Next prepare the cake tin. Cakes stick, even in non-stick tins, so grease the bottom and sides of the tin with margarine (or butter), and cut out a piece of Bakewell paper the size of the bottom of the tin. Put this in place. Then shake about a teaspoonful of flour around the sides of the tin to coat them thoroughly.

If you have a cake tin with a removable base, make certain that there are no gaps between base and tin or you will have puddles of sponge on the oven floor. Cut the base lining paper slightly large to cover the join and thus prevent the cake leaking.

Now measure out the rest of the ingredients and follow the recipe for your particular cake. If you are mixing the cake by hand or in a food mixer, you can prevent the mixture curdling by whisking the eggs in a jug first and adding them to the creamed margarine and sugar in small quantities alternately with teaspoons of the measured flour. An all-in-one cake, e.g. one made by the food processor method, is unlikely to curdle because the eggs and flour are added simultaneously. It takes practice, and luck, to avoid curdling cakes, so if your cake looks like a piece of Gruyère cheese, don't despair – turn to the section on Disasters, Holes Large and Small (p. 127).

When you have mixed the cake, dollop it into the prepared tin, spread it into the corners and flatten the top with the back of a hot wet metal spoon. This should avoid the cake emerging from the oven with a top like an erupting volcano. You are going to turn the cake over to ice because the bottom of the cake is always flat so a few small lumps and bumps on the top won't be seen anyway.

While the cake is cooking, try not to succumb to curiosity. Have the timer set for the minimum time and do not open the oven door before that.

If you do, the cake will probably sink in the middle. If you have an oven with a glass window and a light inside, you can chart your cake's progress without any risk at all; if not, just wait until the timer sounds.

The cake is done when it is a nice golden colour, deeper if it's a chocolate cake, and has shrunk away from the edges of the tin. Press the middle of the cake gently – if the sponge springs back, it is done. If not, pop it back in the oven for five minutes or so. If you are really uncertain, put a skewer or thin bladed knife into the middle of the cake. If it comes out clean, the cake is cooked; if not, put it back for a few minutes.

When you take the cake out of the oven, leave it in its tin for five or ten minutes to cool so that the hot sponge does not crack when turned out of the tin. Turn it out on to a cake rack or something similar. Leave until cold.

If you are following the recipe for a party cake which needs cutting into shape, it is worth freezing or refrigerating the cake before you start carving it up. It is much easier to work on a frozen or chilled cake. Cakes freeze very well and can be stored this way for months if necessary. Refrigerating cakes, however, tends to dry them out so is not satisfactory for more than a day or two's storage. Cover the cake in clingfilm and put it on a flat surface to chill or freeze, making sure that it is not pushed out of shape by other frozen objects. Cakes unfreeze in about two hours, except for big Madeira cakes which take up to four hours.

VICTORIA SPONGE

Food Processor

6 oz (175 gm) softened butter or margarine
6 oz (175 gm) caster sugar
6 oz (175 gm) SR flour
1 tsp baking powder (optional)
3 eggs (size 2)

You can increase the quantities to 4 eggs, 8 oz (225 gm) each of butter, sugar and flour and a generous teaspoonful of baking powder.

Lemon flavour – add the grated rind of a lemon and about 1 tbsp juice.

Orange flavour – add 1 tbsp juice and grated rind of half a medium orange.

Chocolate flavour – for a strong chocolate flavour add 3 level tbsp chocolate powder mixed in to 1½ tbsp hot coffee. Coffee doesn't taste, it just makes the chocolate taste stronger. You can substitute water or orange for coffee. Increase to 4 level tbsp chocolate powder and 2 level tbsp hot coffee for a 4 egg mixture.

This method comes from Tessa Hayward's Magimix Cake Book. Tessa spent lots of time on the phone discussing cake recipes with me and I am very grateful to her.

Set the oven to gas mark 4 (350°F, 180°C).

Use butter so soft it drops off the spoon. (To make the butter really soft, put it in the oven in a basin for a few moments.)

Put the flour and sugar in the Magimix and process for 4 to 5 seconds to aerate the mixture.

Then add the rest of the ingredients and process for 4 seconds. Stop the motor and using a spatula scrape down the sides of the bowl. Then process for 3 seconds. Check that there are no lumps left – if there are, process for another 3 seconds only. Turn into the prepared tins.

Food Mixer

Use the same quantities as for food processor but omit baking powder. This method comes from the Kenwood book and is reliable.

Set the oven at gas mark 5 (375°F, 190°C).

Warm the bowl by filling it with hot water and place the 'K' beater in it while weighing out the ingredients. Mix the fat and the sugar on speed 3 to 4 until combined and then on a higher speed until light and fluffy. Scrape the mixture from the sides of the bowl and beater, and add the eggs one at a time on maximum speed beating to a smooth consistency between each addition. Add a tablespoon of flour with the last egg. Add the remaining flour on speed 1, mixing just long enough to incorporate the flour.

NOTE: I find it best to pour the whisked eggs from a jug, beating in alternate teaspoons of eggs and the measured flour. This way the eggs do not curdle the mixture and it saves time in the long run!

Hand

Use the same quantities as for food processor, omitting baking powder.

Use exactly the same method as for food mixer but substitute your strong right arm for the mixer and 'K' beater. This hand method produced the lightest and best risen cakes so don't despise it! Beat in all the ingredients except for the flour at the end, which should be lightly folded in.

MADEIRA CAKE

Food Processor

This recipe is taken from the Magimix free hand out book and although the texture is not so fine as a real Madeira and much more like a firm Victoria sponge, it is nice, easy and tastes good. It also keeps well and provides a firm base to ice on. It behaves reliably in large quantities. *Do not use this recipe* for cakes which are going to stand up: i.e. Computer, Paddington, Christmas Tree. The cake is not firm enough to stand without buckling. Make the Madeira cake for these by hand or in a mixer using the Kenwood recipe.

8 oz (225 gm) softened butter or margarine
8 oz (225 gm) caster sugar
10½ oz (315 gm) self raising flour
1 tsp Baking Powder
Grated rind and juice of 1 lemon
4 eggs (size 2)

Follow the method for Victoria sponge above and bake for the given time (page 00), at gas mark 3 (300°F, 150°C). Cool slightly in the tin before turning out.

Food Mixer

This recipe comes from the Kenwood book using the 'K' beater.

6 oz (175 gm) softened butter or margarine
6 oz (175 gm) caster sugar
½ grated rind of a lemon
3 eggs (size 2)
8 oz (225 gm) self-raising sponge flour and
½ tsp (2.5 ml) salt sieved together
1 tbsp (20 ml) water

You can increase this recipe very simply by adding one, two or three more eggs and increasing the other ingredients in proportion.

4 eggs
8 oz (225 gm) butter
8 oz (225 gm) sugar
10½ oz (315 gm) SR flour
just over ½ tsp (3 ml) salt
1⅓ tbsp (27 ml) water

5 eggs
10 oz (300 gm) butter
10 oz (300 gm) sugar
13½ oz (405 gm) SR flour
just under 1 tsp (4 ml) salt
1⅔ tbsp (33 ml) water

6 eggs
12 oz (350 gm) butter
12 oz (350 gm) sugar
16 oz (450 gm) SR flour
1 tsp (5 ml) salt
2 tbsp (40 ml) water

Heat oven to gas mark 4 (350°F, 180°C).

Warm the bowl by filling it with hot water and stand the beater in it while weighing out the ingredients. Place the fat and sugar in the bowl with the grated lemon rind. Mix on speed 1 to 2 then on a higher speed as the ingredients combine. Continue until the mixture is light and fluffy. Add the eggs one at a time beating to a smooth consistency between each addition. Add a spoonful of flour with the last egg. Add the flour and the water and mix on speed 1 just long enough to incorporate them into the mixture.

NOTE: To avoid curdling, pour the whisked eggs from a jug, beating in alternate teaspoons of eggs and the measured flour.

Hand

Use the same quantities as for the food mixer method, and make in the same way, beating in all ingredients in the given order but lightly folding in the flour at the end.

COOKING TIMES

It seems evasive to say so but exact cooking times are very difficult to calculate. Ovens vary terrifically both in individual temperament and in the way they are powered. Fan ovens for instance take less time to cook everything and that includes cakes. This can mean up to ten minutes difference and sometimes more. A cook testing recipes in her fan oven took ten minutes less per pair of sandwich cakes for instance than I did in my gas oven.

Cake tins vary as well. Your 2 pint (1.1 litre) pudding basin will hold 2 pints (1.1 litre) but may be a different shape from mine. The golden rule is to consider the depth of the cake – if you are making a 3 egg cake, one inch (2.5 cm) deep, it will take around two thirds the cooking time that the same mixture would take in a smaller deeper cake tin.

So the cooking times which follow should be treated as general guides rather than gospel truth.

Victoria Sponges Cooking times

The following cake mixtures are cooked at gas mark 4 (350°F, 180°C). If you follow the Kenwood recipe however, they suggest you cook at gas mark 5 (375°F, 190°C). When calculating cooking times, therefore, I suggest you take the shorter time for Kenwood recipes and longer for Magimix.

1 to 1½ egg	Pudding basin cake	30 to 40 mins
2 egg	Pudding basin	45 to 55 mins
2 egg	8 inch (20 cm) round (one cake)	30 to 40 mins
3 egg	Pudding basin	65 to 80 mins
3 egg	2 × 8 inch (20 cm) round	25 to 35 mins
3 egg	9 inch (22 cm) round	65 to 75 mins
3 egg	7 to 8 inch (17–20 cm) square	55 to 65 mins
4 egg	2 × 8 inch (20 cm) round	40 to 50 mins
4 egg	7 to 8 inch (17–20 cm) square	65 to 75 mins

Madeira Cooking times

Magimix suggest cooking their recipe for this cake at gas mark 3 (300°F, 150°C), Kenwood at mark 4 (350°F, 180°C). When calculating the cooking time therefore, I suggest you take the shorter time for Kenwood recipes and the longer time for Magimix. Both these times are liable to some variation with individual ovens – unfortunately!

3 egg	7 to 8 inch (17–20 cm) round	70 to 80 mins
3 egg	Shallow roasting tin (e.g. 12 × 6 × 2 inches, 30 × 15 × 5 cm)	80 to 90 min
4 egg	7 to 8 inch (17–20 cm) round	80 to 90 mins
	9 inch (22 cm) round	75 to 85 mins
	10 inch (25 cm) square	65 to 75 mins
5 egg	9 inch (22 cm) round	90 to 105 mins
	10 inch (25 cm) square	90 to 95 mins
6 egg	9 inch (22 cm) round	105 to 115 mins
	10 inch (25 cm) square	100 to 110 mins

ICING THE CAKE

Before starting to ice and decorate the cake, check in the individual recipe whether you need to start by levelling the cake or not. Some require it, others don't. In most cases, you will turn the cake upside down to ice because the original bottom of the cake is flat and regular in shape. The new base of the cake, originally the top, must also be flat and firm so that the cake does not wobble, but it need not be as regularly shaped and smooth as the top.

It is still not too late to fill in any holes so if the top of your cake is pitted and holey, turn to Disasters (p. 127) now.

Before applying the base icing (that is, the flat piece of icing which covers the whole cake and forms the background for the design), set the cake on an icing turntable if you have one – if not use an upturned pudding basin, which I find best, or a soup or dinner plate. The bottom of the cake should stand clear of the basin or plate so that the icing can be trimmed easily. For big square or rectangular cakes, a roasting or biscuit tin slightly smaller than the cake is the most efficient base. Do not use too small a base or the cake will crack and may break in half. When the base icing is on and trimmed, you can remove the cake to a board to finish decorating, if you prefer.

I have used five sorts of icing in this book: fondant, marzipan, butter cream, royal and chocolate yoghourt. (Glacé icing comes under 'Piping', p. 126.) Both fondant and marzipan icings can be bought ready-made and if you live near a supermarket which stocks them, I can see no good reason to make either. The bought versions taste nice, are good value and will save you a lot of time, especially in the case of fondant icing, which can be a real fiddle to make. Some manufacturers produce metric quantities while others stick to Imperial – don't worry too much if you have to buy 250 gm rather than 8 oz: the nearest equivalent will be OK.

You can also buy ready-made mixtures for royal and chocolate icing but I have not tried them and since the other three sorts of icing are quick and simple to make, I haven't bothered to explore alternatives.

Fondant icing

Recipe

1 tbsp liquid glucose, 1 egg white, 1lb 4 oz (500 g) sifted icing sugar.

Take a small jar of liquid glucose and warm it in very hot water. Put 1 tbsp glucose in a deep mixing bowl. Beat in one egg white with a wooden spoon. Add the sifted icing sugar a little at a time, beating well with each addition. Do not be tempted to use a food mixer or processor because air bubbles will then form and never disperse. When your wrist is tired and the icing is stiff, turn it on to a board dredged with some of the remaining icing sugar and knead in the rest. You can bash it about a lot: the more it is kneaded, the whiter and shinier it becomes.

Storage

Do not leave the icing exposed to air before using it because it goes hard; wrap it in a double layer of clingfilm and store it in an airtight box. Knead it well again before use.

Ready-made

I use Whitworths Ready To Roll Fondant icing which is widely available. It received the ultimate accolade when a small girl with a large gap in her front teeth came up to me after eating one of these cakes and told me firmly that 'the ithing tathteth very nithe'.

Uses

I found fondant too fragile to use for modelling figures but it is useful for covering cakes and a marvellous base on which to paint with cake colourings.

Painting

I used small household paint brushes and children's paint brushes to paint the fondant in all sorts of ways. You can even mix the colourings with silver and gold powder to make metallic colours (as for the Butterflies, page 55).

Colouring

You can also use cake colourings to colour fondant in the usual way by mixing the dye with the icing before use. Ordinary cake colourings, available in most supermarkets, are fine for pastel colours, but make the icing too runny when used for strong or deep colours such as bright red, dark brown or black. The best colourings to use for these are the concentrated pastes available from specialist stores such as those listed on page 6.

Whichever sort of colouring you use, add it sparingly with something like a skewer dipped into the dye and then thrust into the icing. Mix it either in an electric mixer, with the beater head attached, or with your hands.

Rolling Out

The best way of rolling out fondant is on a board dredged with a mixture of icing sugar and cornflour, shaken from a flour sifter if you have one but this is not essential. Put the lump of icing on the dredged board and shake more sifted mixture on top. Use a large rolling pin (or milk bottle) to roll out.

Transfer the icing from board to cake with the rolling pin. The cake should already be spread with a thin layer of apricot jam (page 15). Unwrap the icing from the rolling pin and press it gently on to the cake. Rub the iced cake with some dredging mixture which makes the fondant shiny and smooths out any cracks.

Trimming

Trim the fondant at the base of the cake with a very sharp knife. For a really immaculate finish, trim the icing to ⅓ inch (1 cm) deeper than the cake, brush some jam round the inside base of the cake, going in about ⅓ inch (1 cm), and tuck the icing under the cake.

Drying Out

Leave the cake to dry overnight in a cool dry place if you have time, otherwise start decorating.

When you finish decorating the cake, do not cover it with clingfilm – it leaves marks on the icing. The icing will prevent the cake drying out, so you can leave the whole thing somewhere safe and clean to wait for the party.

Freezing

A cake covered with white fondant can be frozen for up to three months. It may look tacky as it thaws but will soon dry out. Coloured fondant and coloured decorations run as they thaw so it is not safe to freeze a decorated cake.

Marzipan

Marzipan comes in two colours, white and yellow, depending on whether you use egg white or yolk as the binding agent.

Recipe

For 1 lb (450 gm) of marzipan. For 8 oz (225 gm) marzipan, halve the quantities.

8 oz (225 gm) ground almonds
4 oz (110 gm) caster sugar
4 oz (110 gm) sieved icing sugar
2 egg whites (for white marzipan) or 2 egg yolks (yellow marzipan)
1 tsp vanilla essence
Rose water or orange flower water (optional)

Mix together the ground almonds and sugar. Add stiffly whisked egg whites or egg yolks to the mixture with the vanilla essence and a few drops of rose water or orange flower water. Mix to a stiff dough.

Storage

Store marzipan double wrapped in clingfilm in an airtight container.

Ready-Made

Ready-made marzipan is available in most stores but smaller shops usually only stock yellow. Do check the recipe carefully before buying yellow marzipan. You cannot colour it as you can white marzipan because it alters the nature of the colour added to it. Where the recipe specifies white, you should not therefore substitute yellow. Make or buy white marzipan.

Use

As well as covering cakes, marzipan is ideal for modelling figures and cutting out shapes because it is stiff and holds its shape well.

Colouring

The basic colouring rules for fondant apply to marzipan (see p. 12). If you find it difficult to buy cake colouring pastes, paint the shapes or models with colouring liquid after making them. You may need to give them two or three coats to get the right depth of colour.

Rolling Out

The easiest way to roll out marzipan is *either* between two sheets of Bakewell paper *or* on a board dredged with a mixture of icing sugar and cornflour with a sheet of Bakewell paper on top of the marzipan. If it wrinkles under the paper, give it a last turn with the rolling pin without the paper.

Cut Out Shapes

Cutting out shapes in marzipan is simple. Lay the template, cut out in Bakewell paper, on the icing. Cut round the shape using a small sharp knife with a wet blade. When the outline is cut out, remove the paper and the surplus marzipan and smooth off any rough edges. Transfer the shape on Bakewell paper to the fridge or freezer to set firm before peeling off the backing paper and placing it on the cake.

ICING THE CAKE

Freezing

Marzipan freezes well once in its life and thaws out easily. If you refreeze it, however, it becomes very clammy when thawing out again and the colours run, so it is wiser not to freeze it more than once.

Butter Icing

I have used butter icing in some of the recipes to coat the sides of the cake. The quantities for this are given in the individual recipes.

You may want to fill a cake with butter icing, and this is a rough guide to the quantities you will need:

7 or 8 inch (18–20 cm) round cake
    2 oz (55 gm) butter or margarine
    4 oz (110 gm) icing sugar
    Flavouring

9 or 10 inch (22–25 cm) round or 8 inch (20 cm) square cake
    3 oz (85 gm) butter or margarine
    6 oz (175 gm) icing sugar
    Flavouring

10 inch (25 cm) square or roasting tin cake
    4 oz (110 gm) butter or margarine
    8 oz (225 gm) icing sugar
    Flavouring

Unsalted butter gives the nicest taste.

I find that the usual proportions of butter to icing sugar (given above) are too sweet for most adults, so I use one part butter to one and a half parts icing sugar (2 oz or 55 gm butter to 3 oz or 85 gm icing sugar, etc.) and lace it well with lemon juice, which gives a much sharper flavour. Do not be tempted to use less sugar than that because it will make the mixture too greasy.

On the other hand, children usually love the very sweet icing so it really depends on whom you are aiming to please at your party. Throughout the book I use the sweeter recipe, and when I refer to, say, a 4 oz/8 oz mixture, it means 4 oz butter or margarine and 8 oz icing sugar.

Flavour butter icing with lemon or orange by adding grated rind and juice to taste. Flavour it chocolate by adding powdered chocolate mixed to a paste with water, orange juice or coffee (see

Top of the Pops cake, page 24). Very often children don't like a strong taste, so add the chocolate mixture sparingly unless your child is a real chocoholic.

Royal Icing

    2 egg whites
    1 lb (450 gm) sieved icing sugar
    2 tsp lemon juice
    2 tsp glycerine (not for every cake, check recipe)

Only use glycerine if the cake is to remain horizontal. It makes the icing soft and slippery, so omit if the cake is going to be vertical or sloping.

Whisk egg whites to a froth. Add lemon juice, and glycerine if used, and then beat in the icing sugar a little at a time until the mixture will stand in peaks. Adjust with more lemon juice or icing sugar if necessary. Cover with a damp cloth, or clingfilm, if not required immediately.

This icing is very easy to make in a food processor or mixer. If you make it by hand, it seems to absorb less icing sugar, so adjust the quantity of icing sugar downwards if using your arm, and upwards if using a food processor.

Spread the icing with a knife dipped in very hot water. Royal icing clings better if you brush a thin layer of apricot jam over the cake surface first.

Chocolate Yoghourt Icing

This is a delicious and easy filling for a chocolate cake such as the Top of the Pops cake on page 24. For a strong taste of chocolate, combine 8 oz (225 gm) of melted plain chocolate with a 9 oz (255 gm) carton of thick Greek yoghourt. This is available at most supermarkets, but you can always substitute sour cream if necessary.

For a less forceful chocolate flavour, reduce the quantity of chocolate by a quarter to a half.

This icing may seem too runny when you make it but it becomes firm quickly.

This quantity will coat and fill a pair of 8 inch (20 cm) sponges, or fill three layers of a 10 inch (25 cm) sponge. To make larger or smaller quantities of icing, increase or decrease the amounts of yoghourt and chocolate in the same ratio.

White Caramel

This is a useful mixture of heated sugar and water which solidifies as it cools.

It takes colouring beautifully but must be removed from the flame before it begins to burn. It is used for the sea in the Ark cake (page 80) and for the lava on the volcano (p. 20).

Put 4 oz (110 gm) of granulated sugar in a heavy-bottomed saucepan containing 4 fl oz (110 ml) of water. Slowly heat the syrup until all the sugar is melted. Turn up the heat a little and cook the caramel until it is thick and bubbling. When it begins to get a 'skin' over the top, it is on the point of turning colour. Remove it from the heat instantly. Handle it very carefully – sugar boils at a very high temperature and it can give a nasty burn.

Pour it over its destination.

To use caramel on a cake board, first cover the board with your choice of back-ground paper, then put a blob of jam in the middle and cover the board with a circle of silver foil. Crinkle the edges up so that the hot caramel cannot flow over them. Leave the caramel to set in a cool place, preferably overnight. Then tear the excess foil from the edge of the caramel – this is very easy.

Meringues

To make 8 large meringues (Space Shuttle cake, p. 103) or 16 smaller ones:

    4 egg whites
    9 oz (255 gm) caster sugar or caster and icing sugar mixed
    Pinch of salt

Whisk the egg whites with the salt in a clean, dry, grease-free bowl. When they are stiff enough to turn the bowl upside down with no disasters, whisk in a quarter of the sugar for about a minute and then lightly fold in the rest until thoroughly blended. Use a spoon or piping bag to dollop the meringue mixture on to a baking sheet covered with Bakewell paper. Cook in a very low oven, about gas mark 2 (275°F, 135°C) until you can lift them off the paper. Store meringues in an airtight container.

Apricot Jam

When you are decorating party cakes, apricot jam is like a universal glue. Its main use is to anchor the icing to the cake, and then to fix the smaller decorations, sweets or silver balls for instance, firmly to the icing.

For most of these cakes, you need the following quantities:

    4 oz (110 gm) of cheapest apricot jam
    2 tbsp water

Heat these together, stirring with a wooden spoon until well mixed, then press through a nylon sieve into a container. Use a pastry brush, or small household paint brush, to spread the sieved jam thinly over the cake before putting on the icing.

Put the jam on smaller decorations with a child's paint brush, or dip the smallest ones, like silver balls, in the jam using a pair of tweezers – the ones with wedge-shaped ends are best. It's easiest to do this if you put a small puddle of jam on a plate. Fix decorations extra firmly if you are taking the cake on a trip – otherwise you may have an awful scrabble in the back of the car for missing decorations.

Paddington Bear

When I was little, there was Rupert Bear, Edward Bear – who was yellow and threadbare and, as far as I was concerned, belonged to my brother – and Winnie the Pooh. Now, my godson Rory tells me, there is really only Paddington Bear and he is 'best'!

This cake is easy to make but allow yourself two hours to do so. A square sponge is carved in the shape of Paddington and iced with his clothes! You will have some pieces of sponge left over which can be iced or used for trifle.

This Bear cake can stand upright as he does in the photograph, but you must then make his suitcase smaller or the weight will make him topple forwards.

It should feed about 14 people. You could easily decorate it the night before the party and leave it in a cool place.

YOU WILL NEED:

CAKE 9 inch (22 cm) square Madeira sponge made with a 4 or 5 egg mixture (*Not* made in food processor if it has to stand up)

ICING 1½ lb (675 gm) yellow marzipan
4 oz (110 gm) fondant (buy an 8 oz (225 gm) block)

JAM 6 oz (175 gm) warm, sieved apricot jam

COLOURINGS Red, light blue, dark blue, brown paste

DECORATIONS Small packet of chocolate chips or Polka Dots (currants if desperate)
2 small packets of chopped, mixed nuts or similar

CAKE BOARD 14 inch (35 cm) square cake board

OPTIONAL Paddington Station sign
London transport poster
Shiny yellow wrapping paper

It is easier to use a semi-frozen or chilled cake for this.

Level up the cake, turn it over and put it on a big board.

Trace the outline of Paddington Bear from the stencil on to a piece of Bakewell paper and cut round it. Put the stencil on the cake, push down firmly with a sharp knife and cut out the bear. It is easiest if you look straight down on the cake rather than doing it from an angle.

Brush the whole cake with melted jam.

Roll out the marzipan, cut out the Paddington shape and cover the top of the cake.

Trim neatly and save the pieces.

Set the cake aside for the moment and cut up the Paddington outline into the following pieces:

Crown of hat

Brim of hat × 2

Jacket including lapels and cuffs

Wellington boots

Leave two small pieces of yellow marzipan, the size of walnuts, for his hands and his suitcase.

Colour the rest bright red. Roll out the marzipan thinly. On top of it, lay the patterns for his hat and boots and cut round, using a small knife dipped in very hot water. Remember you need two brim pieces so that the brim appears raised. Don't throw away the bits of red marzipan, they come in useful later.

Brush the pieces of marzipan with jam and fix them in place on the cake.

Colour the fondant icing light blue. Lay the whole jacket pattern, including collar and cuffs, on the blue icing and cut out. Paint Paddington's arms and body with jam and lay his jacket in place.

Colour the remaining light blue fondant dark blue. Roll it out and cut out the collar and cuffs, using the bits from the main pattern. Brush with jam and put in position.

Make impressions on the jacket to indicate arm lines with the handle of a teaspoon dipped in very hot water.

Now for his suitcase. Cut out the rectangle from the stencil. Dye the piece of yellow marzipan dark brown, and cover a rectangle of leftover cake the same size as the pattern. Brush the back of the suitcase with jam and fix firmly on to the cake. Make initials and handle with tiny sausages of red marzipan.

Take the other piece of yellow marzipan and make two little flat ovals for his paws. Put them on the cake so that he looks as if he is clasping his suitcase.

Finally, brush the side of his face with a little jam and stick a few chopped nuts on there to resemble whiskers. Push in two chocolate chips for his eyes, with the points outwards. Push in one chip for his nose, with the point inwards. Use a piece of red apple skin or some leftover red marzipan to make a smiling mouth and fix it on with some jam.

The finishing touch is to brush apricot jam over the sides of the cake, and press chopped nuts all over them.

Erupting Volcano (with Fleeing Dinosaurs)

Benjamin Georget asked me to make this cake for his eighth birthday party. Originally he had asked me to make a space cake, but a few days before the party, his mother rang and stuttered down the phone, 'You won't believe this but Benjamin is now having a Prehistoric Party and he wants an erupting volcano with fleeing dinosaurs.'

I was so taken aback that I couldn't say anything, let alone yes. They persuaded me that this was a real challenge – I hate challenges – and I should have a stab at it because I was doing this book, wasn't I? The only good news was that I didn't have to make the dinosaurs. Every toyshop has a selection of dinosaurs and other prehistoric monsters.

I was very busy at the time of his birthday and went on strike about making the actual cakes. This volcano was made with three cakes, stacked on top of each other, with a hole scooped out of the top, where the lava comes from, and I bought them from a well-known store with a good food department.

It doesn't matter what combination of cakes you use, but you want to aim at a pyramid of cake with a hole in the middle. You could use a ring mould and bake the top in that, and put it on top of a slightly larger deep Madeira. Cut away the sides of whatever cakes you use to produce a cone effect.

The lava is reddened caramel and the really sinister seething mass at the top is caramel gone wrong. All good cookery books tell you on no account to let the sugar in the caramel crystallise because it forms this sort of bubbly crust. It is simply a question of stirring the caramel vigorously every so often and letting it

cook for a long time. The result is ideal for this purpose and it's great fun doing something wrong.

Benjamin's mother bought an enormous quantity of chocolate 'rubble' to lie at the bottom of the volcano – about 3 lb (1.3 kg). Benjamin's parents and I made the cake between 10.30 and midnight on the evening before his party and we had a wonderful time.

It should be left in a cold place overnight because of all the chocolate.

Nothing is precise about this cake – more or less of this or that is fine so regard this as an approximate guide to quantities.

YOU WILL NEED:

CAKE 2 or 3 cakes, bought or homemade making a total height of about 6 to 8 inches (15–20 cm) high and 8 to 10 inches (20–25 cm) wide at the base. Pudding basins or ring moulds are good for the top.

ICING 1 lb (450 gm) chocolate cake covering
2 lbs (900 gm) white marzipan

CARAMEL 8 oz (225 gm) granulated sugar and 8 fl oz (225 ml) water

JAM 6 oz (175 gm) warm, sieved apricot jam

COLOURING Red

DECORATIONS 2 to 3 lbs (900 gm–1.3 kg) assorted chocolate rocks, shells, mini-flakes, Maltesers, chocolate truffles, raisins, prunes, dates, and popcorn
2 oz (60 gm) granulated sugar for scree

EXTRAS 14 inch (35 cm) square cake board
Artificial grass to cover board
Fat red candle
Indoor sparklers
Red and yellow birthday candles and holders
Optional dinosaurs

First of all, put the caramel to cook. If you are worried about making caramel, don't be – if it goes wrong, it's better. Melt the sugar and water slowly in a heavy-bottomed saucepan. Don't bother to stir it, at this stage. Add some red colouring until it is a good colour – by the time the caramel has browned a bit, it will be darker anyway. Let the caramel go on cooking while you get on with the rest. Look at it every so often to make certain it is getting thicker but not burning too much – you should avoid making toffee.

Warm the apricot jam – you really don't have to sieve it for this cake. Sandwich the three cakes together with some of the jam. Cut the cakes into a cone shape. Scoop a shallow hole out of the top one for the lava and the red candle.

Coat the pyramid of cakes with the rest of the jam.

Very roughly roll out the marzipan and start by lining the hole at the top and then work your way down the sides of the volcano. Make it knobbly and rough. Form big boulders and gullies at the bottom where the volcano will hit the grass.

Line the base of the crater with foil and set a fat red candle in it. The picture shows small candles, but these are more effective set around the top.

Cover the board with the fake grass and put the cake on it.

Melt the chocolate with 2 tbsp water until it is warm and runny and pour it over the cake.

Sprinkle the 2 oz (55 gm) quantity of granulated sugar over the knobbly bits of the volcano to look like scree.

Arrange the pounds of different chocolates around the bottom of the cake and put the dinosaurs in suitable positions, fleeing from the encroaching lava.

The caramel should be approaching lava stage now. When it begins to get thick and turn brown round the edges, take it off the heat. You must make certain it is really thick, or it will not set properly. If you are uncertain, drop a blob in some cold water: if it forms a ball, it is done. If it doesn't, cook it a bit more. It doesn't matter if the caramel turns brown right through, the red colouring will keep it the right sort of lava colour.

Pour the lava round the candles in the crater and down the sides and front of the volcano. When you have used half to two thirds of the caramel, put it back on the stove and let it crystallise. Then pour it all on the top and down the front of the volcano. The children were thrilled that the dinosaurs had lava on their tails – it added greatly to the tenseness of the situation.

When it is time for the party, put sparklers all round the volcano and candles on the top. Light all the candles. Try and carry the cake into a dark room, or put the cake in a room with the lights off and the curtains drawn so that the children only see the volcano when it is alight. The shrieks and screams of delight are well worth the stage management.

Top of the Pops

I made this cake for eleven-year-old Nimrata Budrani, who is mad about pop music and chocolate cakes. She asked for the 'chocolatiest' cake I could make and this one is a real taste sensation for chocolate fanciers. I was worried in case it was too sweet and heavy, so I used chocolate and orange butter icing on the outside and chocolate yoghourt icing (p. 14) to fill the cake.

The cake mixture has a high liquid content and keeps very well wrapped up in a cool place. You may be alarmed if you look through the oven window while the cake is cooking, because it tends to billow upwards, but it does settle down again and gives a nice flat top to work on. The coffee which is used to melt the chocolate doesn't really taste, it just seems to give a richer chocolate flavour.

If you like piping, pipe the letters in glacé icing.

The colour scheme could be varied to suit your child's taste. Nimrata wanted chocolate and pink so the record label was pink and the lettering gold. This cake will give you at least 24 thick gooey slices.

YOU WILL NEED:

CAKE 2 chocolate sponges, each made with a 3 egg mixture and baked in 9–10 inch (22–25 cm) round tins

ICING Chocolate butter icing made with 6 oz (175 gm) unsalted butter, 9–12 oz (255–335 gm) of sieved icing sugar (taste for sweetness), the grated rind of one medium orange, and 6 oz (175 gm) chocolate powder dissolved in the warm juice of the orange (p. 14).
Chocolate yoghourt icing made with 1 small tub of Greek yoghourt (8½ oz/ 240 gm) and 6–8 oz (175–225 gm) good quality plain chocolate (depending on how strong you want it – see p. 14).
8 oz (225 gm) white marzipan for letters

COLOURINGS Paste or liquid in two colours, e.g. pink and gold

DECORATIONS Coloured balls (dragées) Chocolate vermicelli

EXTRAS 14 inch (35 cm) round cake board
Pink or other wrapping paper
Candles and candleholders

You will need tweezers and a paint brush for this cake
Keep this cake in a cool place

Cut the two big cakes in half sideways, using a long knife with a serrated edge (a bread or ham knife is perfect). Fill the three layers with the chocolate yoghourt icing.

Now make the record label. Take 1½ oz (45 gm) of marzipan and dye it pink. Roll it out to about ¼ inch (0.5 cm) thickness and cut out a circle about 3 inches (7.5 cm) wide. You could use a cutter if you have one, but a wine glass will do. Brush the back of the circle with jam and fix in the middle of the cake.

Using the stencils on page 122 as a guide, cut out NO. 1 in marzipan letters. Paint these gold and when dry fix on to the label with a little jam.

Use coloured marzipan worms to make 'Happy Birthday' and the child's name. You can colour these gold and silver or even mix a colour and gold or silver to make a stunning metallic finish. Put the letters on one side or in the freezer to firm up.

If you prefer to pipe the message, do so when the top of the cake is iced.

Take the butter icing and put a thinnish coating on the sides of the cake. Before you ice the top, coat the sides with chocolate vermicelli. Set the cake on its board on a big tray (to catch the falling surplus vermicelli). Use a small knife with a fat blade to lift the vermicelli on to the side of the cake – load the knife, put the bottom edge against the cake and quickly push the blade against it. The vermicelli clings very easily, but this is a messy business.

Now coat the top of the cake with the rest of the butter icing. Use a fork to make circular grooves in the icing so that it looks like a record. Be careful not to get the butter icing over the pink record label. It is a good idea to mask the label with the cutter or wine glass. When you have marked the top, put a row of silver and coloured balls round the label, next to the butter icing.

Now take the Happy Birthday letters and the child's name and arrange them round the top of the cake.

Using tweezers, dip silver and coloured balls in jam and press them into the side of the cake in the shape of notes of music, on the chocolate vermicelli background.

Put candles in holders around the outside of the cake.

Keep this cake in a cool place overnight. If you use porous paper on the cake board rather than foil, put the cake on the board just before the party: it is so gooey that it may discolour the paper.

Pink Elephant

I made this cake for Jessica Cran's first birthday party. She has a wonderful pair of dungarees with an elephant on the bib, which gave me the idea for the cake.

When I was little, I was devoted to a book about a pink baby elephant, whose ears were so big that they acted as wings. This one has very big ears and I thought he would look charming against a background of blue sky and white clouds.

Jessie had a very sophisticated birthday party: she and Mark Hanington, also aged 1, were the only people under thirty. It has to be said that neither of them seemed to be terrifically interested in eating the cake although they enjoyed pulling bits off and trying to blow out the magic candle. Anyway, the grown ups more than made up for

them and fell upon the cake with glee, one rather crusty bachelor saying, as he put a large piece in his mouth, 'My goodness, this is a work of art!'

The work of art was chocolate sponge and the middle was filled with chocolate butter icing, but you can make it lemon or orange if you prefer.

The elephant's tail was a handy carnation, one of those small ones that I always think are pinks. You don't, of course, have to use the same flower, anything remotely similar would be fine; you could even use a lollipop. This cake takes about 1½ hours to decorate and will give about 16 slices.

YOU WILL NEED:

CAKES 2 Victoria sponges baked in 8 inch (20 cm) straight-sided tins from a 4 egg mixture

ICING 1½ lb (675 gm) white fondant or 1 lb (450 gm) white fondant and 8 oz (225 gm) white marzipan
Butter icing made with 4 oz/8 oz (110/225 gm) mixture flavoured as cake (see p. 14)

JAM 4 oz (110 gm) warm sieved apricot jam

COLOURINGS Pink and blue liquid or paste
   Silver non-toxic poster paint or powder
DECORATIONS Flower for tail
   Pink and silver balls (dragées)
EXTRAS Cake board and pale blue wrapping
   paper
   Candles and holders

*You will need tweezers and a paint brush
for this cake*

It is much easier to cut out the elephant
from a frozen or chilled sponge. If the
cake is not frozen at the start, wrap one
sponge carefully in clingfilm and put
it in the freezer or fridge for half an
hour. You can cover the cake board
and start making the sky cake.

It does not matter at all if the sponges
are a bit lopsided – just position them
with the higher side at the back. If they
have risen gently in the middle, that
is fine, but if they actually come to a
peak in the middle level them off.

Split one sponge and fill it with half
the butter icing. Don't spread the
filling right out to the edge. If you do,
it will splurge down the sides when
you come to put the top on.

Put the top back and push it firmly
down. Put the cake on an upturned
dinner plate or basin.

Take 8 oz (225 gm) of fondant and
colour it pale sky blue. Roll it out and
cover the filled cake. Trim and set
aside.

Take another 8 oz (225 gm) of
fondant, roll it out and cut lots of
different sized white clouds. Use a
round cutter or glass, about 2½ inches
(6 cm) in diameter, to make the basic
circles, then cut them into cloud
shapes using a small sharp knife.

Use a tiny piece of icing to make a
tusk, about ¾ inch (1.5 cm) long and just
less than ¼ inch (0.5 cm) wide.

Take another scrap of icing for his
tongue and paint it deep pink.

For his eye, use a tiny triangle of
icing, painted silver. The sides of the
triangle should be about ⅓ inch (just
under 1 cm) long. When it is dry,
push a silver ball into the middle.

Put clouds, tusk, tongue and eye on
one side to dry on a sheet of Bakewell
paper.

Now take the other sponge out of
the freezer. Copy the stencil of the
elephant on to Bakewell paper. Lay it
on top of the sponge, and cut round
with a small sharp knife. Split the cake
and fill it with the remaining butter
icing, mounding it up towards the back
of the cake so that the elephant's
backbone is higher than his feet.

Take off the stencil and brush the
elephant shape with jam.

Colour the remaining 8 oz (225 gm)
of fondant or marzipan pale pink. Roll
it out. Using the ear from the elephant

stencil, cut the shape out from the icing and paint it a slightly deeper pink round the edge so that it shows up. Leave it on one side on a sheet of Bakewell paper. Lay the rest of the icing on top of the elephant cake. Press down gently on top and round the sides.

The only tricky bit is the trunk. Do the side facing you first – that's what people will see! Then make a slit in the icing from top to bottom of the corner at the base of his head and his trunk. This should enable you to push the icing gently down the side of his trunk and forehead. Ease the icing down and round the cake so that it covers up any

gaps. Don't worry if it doesn't – you can always patch it up from the leftovers.

Make a slit in the icing between his front and back feet and tuck it in. It is only meant to be a suggestion of a gap, so don't bother trying to do more.

Trim the icing from the base with a sharp knife and patch up any holes that show around the back of his trunk. Don't forget that the icing sugar/ cornflour mixture will smooth out most cracks and joins.

With the handle of a slim teaspoon or something similar – I use an old-fashioned butter knife – make lines to indicate the elephant's legs.

Using tweezers, dip the pink and silver ball bearings in a shallow puddle of apricot jam and push into place as toenails.

Fix his tusk, ear, tongue and eye in place with a spot of jam.

With a narrow paint brush, paint silver eyelashes round this heffalump's eye.

Put the pink elephant on his blue cloud and then put the whole cake on the board, which you have covered with sky blue paper. Position the clouds around the base of the cake and on to the board.

Tuck a flower into the elephant for his tail and just before you put the cake on the table, put a candle and holder in the top of his trunk.

And that is all there is to a work of art.

Snowman

As an alternative Christmas cake, or for someone whose birthday is near snow time, you could make this easy Snowman cake. You could make either the bottom half or the whole snowman in fruit cake if you prefer. This snowman is a happy chap looking blithely contented with his chilly lot. He is very, very easy to make and should only take you about an hour to decorate. The easiest way is to make the cakes two days before the party, ice them the day before, leave the icing to dry out overnight and put on the hat, scarf and buttons on the day of the party. You could, of course, make the cakes early on the day before the party and ice them later the same day. You will get 30 or more rather strange shaped slices from this cake.

Be careful of the cocktail sticks when children are eating the cake.

<u>YOU WILL NEED:</u>

CAKE 2 × 3 egg Victoria sponges, baked in 2 pint (1.1 litre) pudding basins 2 × 1 egg Victoria sponges baked in 1 pint (0.6 litre) pudding basins (make a 2 egg mixture and divide it)

ICING 1½ lb (675 gm) Royal icing mixture made with 3 egg whites, 1½ tbsp lemon juice, 1½ lb (675 gm) sieved icing sugar (p. 14)
1½ lb (675 gm) marzipan to cover cake
8 oz (225 gm) white marzipan for nose, scarf and hat
3 oz/6 oz (85/175 gm) quantity lemon butter icing (p. 14)

JAM 4 to 6 oz (110–175 gm) warm, sieved apricot jam

DECORATIONS Tube of Smarties
Small packet of Cadbury's Chocolate Buttons

COLOURINGS Red, black and orange liquid or paste

EXTRAS 14 inch (35 cm) round cake board
Cocktail stick
Green paper
Candles and holders
Sprig of holly

Stand all four cakes pointed ends down on a flat board and make certain that the tops are flat and level – trim them with a sharp knife if not.

Sandwich the big pair of pudding basin cakes flat sides together with two thirds of the butter icing to make the spherical body. Use the rest to

sandwich together the small pair of cakes in the same way for his head. Put each sphere on an upturned pudding basin.

Make sure the butter icing is not oozing out and brush the cakes with a thin layer of jam. Roll out 1½ lbs (675 gm) marzipan thinly to cover both pairs of cakes; cover the body first and then reroll the marzipan thinly and cover the head. Keep any surplus marzipan. Put both cakes aside on Bakewell paper.

Cover the cake board with green or white paper and dust with preserving sugar to look like snow.

Put the big cake on the cake board; leave the small one on some Bakewell paper.

Use any surplus marzipan to wedge round the base of the snowman to keep him absolutely steady.

Brush both cakes with a thin layer of apricot jam.

Make the Royal icing and use a palette knife to spread the icing over both parts of the snowman. Turn the cakes to make sure you cover them evenly. Leave to dry overnight.

Last thing today, colour about ½ oz (15 gm) of the white marzipan bright orange and form into a carrot shape about 1½ inches (3.5 cm) long. Leave on a piece of Bakewell paper to dry.

If the Royal icing slips a bit on the cakes, don't worry. Just scoop it up and plaster it back again.

On the day of the party, jam the head well down on the body. If it looks really insecure, push a long skewer through his crown down to his body to hold him in place. The handle of the skewer is hidden by the hat and holly.

Colour half the remaining marzipan bright red, use a 2 inch (5 cm) worm for his mouth and fix on with jam. Roll out the rest between sheets of Bakewell paper and make a scarf about 1 inch (2.5 cm) wide and 20 inches (50 cm) long – it is easiest to roll out a piece 10 × 2 inches (25 × 5 cm) and slit it down the middle, joining the two ends together at the back of the snowman's neck.

Colour the rest of the marzipan black and roll it out to a rough circle. Don't bother to trim the edges, just push it on to his head. Pull the crown up a little and push the brim around to make it look like an old hat.

Push the buttons in for his eyes, the Smarties or more buttons down his front, and make a hole for his carrot nose, anchoring the nose with a cocktail stick to secure it. Push the sprig of holly into his hat.

Marshmallow Garden

*T*his cake is a Marshmallow Garden if you have some time to spend on it, and a Lollipop Garden if you don't. Either way, it is very simple to make and children love it.

I made it for Kate Pakenham's un-Birthday because I missed her real one. Kate and her friend Alexandra are blowing out the candles in the picture. It is a very pretty cake and probably most suitable for a birthday girl, especially if you decorate the table in pink, green and white.

It will take you about one and a half hours to decorate and will feed 12 to 16 children.

YOU WILL NEED:

CAKE Two 7 or 8 inch (17 or 20 cm) chocolate sponges (or plain if you prefer) from a 3 or 4 egg mixture.

ICING 4 oz/8 oz (110/225 gm) quantity chocolate butter icing (p. 14)
8 oz (225 gm) white marzipan

JAM 4 oz (110 gm) warm, sieved apricot jam

COLOURINGS Blue and green, liquid or paste

DECORATIONS 1 packet of sweet popcorn – about 4 oz (110 gm)
1 packet of Cadbury's Chocolate Buttons – about 4 oz (110 gm)
1 drum hundreds and thousands
1 box long Matchmakers or Chocolate Peppermint Sticks
1 packet of marshmallows
1 small drum of angelica
1 packet of chocolate Polka Dots
8 oz (225 gm) Dolly Mixture
12 large lollipops if you are using lollipops and not marshmallow trees. (If you can't get any of these, don't worry – any similar sorts of sweets will do.)
Blue jelly, made with ¼ pt (150 ml) water, blue colouring and peppermint flavouring

EXTRAS 14 inch (35 cm) square cake board
Cake candles and holders
Chocolate ladybirds, tortoises and other animals

Keep this cake in the fridge

Use frozen or unfrozen cakes for this recipe.

Take one cake and put it on an upturned dinner plate.

Cut a round about 2½ to 3 inches (7–8 cm) in diameter from the centre of the cake. Brush the cake with jam.

Colour the white marzipan green

and roll it out so that it will cover the whole cake. Lay it on the cake and trim round the edges. Slit the marzipan over the well in the middle and push it down the sides.

Make the blue jelly and put it to set in the fridge.

Brush the board with apricot jam and scatter hundreds and thousands thickly over it.

Brush the pieces of popcorn with jam and stick round the edge of the board. Repeat with the chocolate buttons.

Put the green cake in the centre of the board. Surround the well or pond with pieces of upright angelica about ½ inch (1 cm) high to look like reeds and put the candles round it.

Cut a hole about 3 inches (7 cm) in diameter from the middle of the second cake and then cut the outer ring into four quarters. These are the flower beds.

Cover the flower beds thickly with butter icing. Press chocolate Polka Dots around the sides. Cut four strips of green marzipan to fit the short sides of the flower beds, about 2½ inches (6 cm) long, spread them with jam and dust thickly with hundreds and thousands. Brush the undersides with jam and stick on to the flower beds, as paths.

Cut up some more angelica and put on the top edges of the flower beds. Then arrange a quarter of the Dolly Mixture in each flower bed and put some of the small lollipops in the middle. Lift the flower beds with a fish slice and put them in position on the board.

Now make the marshmallow trees, if you are using them. With the blade of a small knife, make a hole in the side of the marshmallow. Push in a long Matchmaker. Take two small blobs of leftover green marzipan and press them into long oval shapes. Fix them on either side of the marshmallow tree with jam. Make up the packet of marshmallows in this way – about 24 in all. Put these on a flat base in the fridge. Don't be tempted to put them on the cake until less than an hour before the party. And don't put them in the freezer, the marzipan cracks horribly.

An hour or so before the party, fill the well with chopped-up blue jelly. Put the marshmallow trees or lollipops around the green cake, fixing them with jammy green marzipan. Put the cake in a cool place until it is time to serve it – floppy marshmallow trees are not the same as upright ones!

The Greedy Tiger

*T*his is a bouncing, good-tempered, Tigger sort of tiger – romping in an emerald forest. He has spotted a smug parrot sitting on a branch just above him eating a banana. This type of tiger likes bananas so he is reaching up with his great big stripey paws to see if he can just manage to make a bit of fruit drop in his direction. A very vague butterfly is watching detachedly – butterflies don't eat fruit – and a bronze serpent half as old as Time thinks these young things are very silly – haven't they discovered that lollipop trees are much more exciting and delicious than boring bananas? Max Webster (page 4) has ordered this cake for his fourth birthday in December 1986 because 'it has a moving tiger' and it is one of my great favourites. It is very simple to make and you can do the whole thing easily in an afternoon or evening. It will feed 16 to 20 children.

NOTE Please don't worry if you cannot buy the exact sweets I have used – any chocolates that look like stones and trees, and any jellies or similar sweets that look like jungle fruit, will do beautifully.

<u>YOU WILL NEED:</u>

CAKE 9 or 10 inch (22–25 cm) square Madeira made with a 5 or 6 egg mixture

ICING 4 oz/8 oz (110 gm/225 gm) mixture butter cream icing, flavoured lemon and tinted bright green (p. 14)
2 oz/4 oz (55 gm/110 gm) mixture butter cream icing, flavoured with chocolate to your taste (p. 14)
8 oz (225 gm) white or yellow marzipan

JAM 1 oz (30 gm) warm, sieved apricot jam

COLOURINGS Black, orange, scarlet, blue, yellow, green paste or liquid
Non-toxic gold paint or gold powder

DECORATIONS 4–6 oz (110–175 gm) assorted jungle chocolates (round, oval, pebbly)
½ oz (15 gm) currants or raisins
1 oz (30 gm) angelica, cut into short thin pieces
Coloured balls
2 to 3 oz (55–85 gm) tree and branch chocolates (I used Matchmakers and chocolate-covered Orange Sticks)

8 to 10 large nuts, e.g. pecan or walnuts
8 to 10 yellow or coloured jellies
8 to 10 lollipops – any colours
I bought a tub of marzipan fruit
containing a banana 1 inch (2.5 cm)
long (make this if you cannot buy it)

*You will need tweezers and a paint brush
for this cake*

You do not need to use a frozen cake
for this recipe. I made the marzipan
cut-outs whilst the cake was in the
oven.

   Cut out the tiger stencil in two
pieces, body and tail. Roll out the
marzipan thickly to about 1/5 inch (0.5
cm) and cut out the two shapes. Cut
out the butterfly (stencil page 56). Cut
out the parrot stencil twice and stick the
two pieces together with jam, one on

top of the other. Roll the rest of the marzipan into a fat serpent about 7 or 8 inches (17.5–20 cm) long, and bend his body in wiggles with his head pointing up.

Now paint the shapes as illustrated in the photograph. You need to paint the tiger orange all over and let that dry before painting on the black stripes. Make his mouth groove with the wrong end of a pair of tweezers, or similar, and paint it bright red – he should look eager and beamish. Use a green ball for his eye. The butterfly is painted in scarlet and deep pink and decorated with silver balls. Leave this to dry with one wing propped up on crumpled foil or Bakewell paper. Paint the parrot bright blue, scarlet and yellow and give him a silver ball eye. Paint the serpent gold, and when the paint is dry, stud his spine with metallic balls and push in two extra for his eyes.

Leave all the creatures to dry on Bakewell paper.

When the cake is completely cold, look at it as a diamond and cover the bottom quarter with chocolate icing. Fork this from side to side. Cover the rest with bright green butter icing and fork this up and down. This use of chocolate horizontal and emerald vertical fork lines creates an instant effect of paths and trees. Cover the chocolate icing with the assorted chocolates and currants. Set the body of the tiger on the green icing so that he is reaching upwards and then put the parrot on a branch just above his nose. Let the parrot hold the banana in his claw. If you were not able to buy a little tub of marzipan fruit, form a curved banana from marzipan. If you use white marzipan, paint it yellow and when that is dry, paint a few brown streaks and spots. Position the butterfly at top left.

Now finish off the cake by making lollipop trees from tree sort of chocolates, like Matchmakers, and the eight lollipops.

Make nut and jelly trees on the other side from tree chocolates, big nuts and coloured jellies. Join the tiger's tail to his body and curl it round and over the tree trunks. Put the serpent on the jungle path, with his head pointing up a lollipop tree. Then take the pieces of angelica and stick them at the base of the emerald forest where it hits the path.

I found the best background for this colourful cake is plain gold, but yellow would do well, or chocolate brown. We 'borrowed' the lions and tigers from the ark (p. 80) for the photograph and they fit in very well as interested parties if you have time to make them.

Teddy Bear Diary

This teddy bear, who has no name so far, was the result of an afternoon's doodling with Bryan Kemp, a friendly graphic designer. Despite his anonymity, he has become a great favourite with my friends and we decided that he deserved a cake to himself as well as his prominent position on the cover.

You could easily adapt any cartoon animal or character to use in this way – Snoopy, Garfield, Mickey Mouse – or copy a character from a book, such as Postman Pat. Just find an illustration the right size, trace an outline in Bakewell paper and follow this recipe.

Diaries are often spiral bound and I was trying to give this diary cake an authentic look when I made a most exciting discovery – halved

Polo Mints look exactly like spiral binding!

I made the cake in a shallow roasting tin, measuring 12 × 10 × 2 inches (30 × 25 × 5 cm) but the exact dimensions don't matter at all: you could use any tin approximately the same size. You can make this cake very quickly and you don't need to freeze it before icing. You could bake the cake and ice it in an afternoon with no trouble.

It will feed about 16 people.

<u>YOU WILL NEED:</u>

CAKE 4 egg Madeira sponge cake made in a 10 × 12 inch (25 × 30 cm) roasting tin or something similar

ICING 8 oz (225 gm) yellow marzipan
8 oz (225 gm) fondant
Butter icing made with 2 oz (55 gm) margarine, 4 oz (110 gm) icing sugar, 1 tbsp lemon juice (p. 14)

JAM 4 oz (110 gm) warm, sieved apricot jam

COLOURINGS Red, blue, green, yellow liquid or paste

DECORATIONS Packet of Polo Mints
Hundreds and thousands
Small quantity of chocolate vermicelli
1 currant or raisin
Coloured balls (dragées)

EXTRAS Cake board to fit cake
    Paper to cover
    Candles and holders

PIPING If you decide to pipe the lettering
    you will need a 4 oz (110 gm) quantity
    of glacé icing (p. 126) and a piping bag
    with a small nozzle.

While the big cake is cooking, roll out the yellow marzipan and use the stencil to cut out the teddy bear and his cake. Put them on a sheet of Bakewell paper. Cut out the extra piece of cake and fix it on top of the first with jam. Paint the small cake with jam and dredge it with hundreds and thousands. Put the cake in place by the bear.

Now cut out the extra pieces of teddy bear: his ear, arms and legs. Fix them on with jam, positioning his arm so that he looks as if he is holding the cake.

Then cut out his neck bow and band and paint them bright blue. Leave them on Bakewell paper to dry and then fix in place with jam.

Brush a little jam on his feet and push in some chocolate vermicelli to look like the soles of his feet.

Make a groove for his mouth with the back of a pair of tweezers or something like that, and paint his

mouth bright red. Use a scrap of marzipan painted red for his tongue, and fix it on with jam. Push a green ball in for his eye and half a currant or raisin for his nose.

Put the teddy bear on Bakewell paper in the freezer or fridge, to set firm before you transfer him to the cake.

Now turn to the main cake. When it is completely cold, cut it into two equal rectangles. Brush the tops with apricot jam. Lay the pieces of cake on a board to ice: do not use an upturned plate because the cake may crack.

Colour the marzipan green and lay it on the top of the right hand cake. You don't need to cover the sides. Trim neatly. Wrap the trimmings in clingfilm to use later for lettering. Roll out the fondant, cut out the bear's speech balloon and fix it on the right hand page with a blob of jam.

Roll out the rest of the fondant and lay it on the top of the left hand page. Trim the sides and save the bits for lettering. Wrap them tightly in clingfilm.

Paint the fondant a watery red and leave to dry.

Rescue the teddy bear from the freezer or fridge, and fix him in place on the cake with a little blob of jam.

Now spread the sides of the cakes with butter icing, forked sideways to look like pages of a book. You only need to coat one of the middle sides. Lift the two cakes gently with a fish slice and put them together on the cake board. Push them together in the middle.

With a sharp knife, cut five Polo Mints in half and put them curved side up over the centre join to look like spiral binding – my favourite bit!

By now the red fondant icing should be dry and you can do the lettering on the left hand page. It is entirely up to you which way you do the lettering. You could pipe it all if you are good at piping, or make it all out of fondant, or some out of fondant and some out of marzipan. The lettering illustrated is made up of white fondant for 'Tuesday', piped green glacé icing for 'Edward's', and piped white glacé icing for 'Party' studded with coloured balls for fun.

I piped 'Happy Birthday Edward' in green glacé icing on the speech balloon but you could equally well paint it with a fine paint brush and black or green colouring paste.

Finally, push three candles into the teddy bear's cake and put the rest around the big cake.

The End of the Rainbow

The myth about the crock of gold at the end of the rainbow actually comes true with this cake. There are plenty of gold coins spilling around but, as a little extra, it would be nice to give each child one of those little sacks of coins as a party present.

I made a great discovery when I first made this cake — new to me if not to seasoned cake decorators. Thinking it was far too much of a fiddle to cut out all the colours of the rainbow separately, I cut out a big piece of marzipan and tried painting it with the cake dyes. It works beautifully and is very quick and easy.

If you prefer, you could also paint the fondant which covers the whole cake rather than mixing the colour with the icing

before applying it. The photograph shows the background icing coloured beforehand and not painted, but if you would like to paint it, use the instructions given for the Black Beauty horse (page 50).

This cake should not take more than two hours to decorate and will feed 12 to 16 people.

<u>YOU WILL NEED:</u>

CAKE 7 inch (17 cm) square Victoria or Madeira made with 3 or 4 eggs

ICING 1 lb (450 gm) fondant icing
8 oz (225 gm) white marzipan

JAM 4 oz (110 gm) sieved warm apricot jam

COLOURINGS Red, orange, yellow, green, blue, black, violet liquid colour

DECORATIONS Silver balls
Bags of gold chocolate coins

CAKE BOARD 12 or 14 inch (30 or 35 cm) square cake board and dark blue paper

You will need tweezers and a paint brush for this cake

You don't need to use a frozen cake for this recipe. If the cake is uneven, even it up as much as possible, turn it upside down and put it on an upturned dinner plate. Brush it with warm apricot jam.

Colour half the fondant icing pale blue.

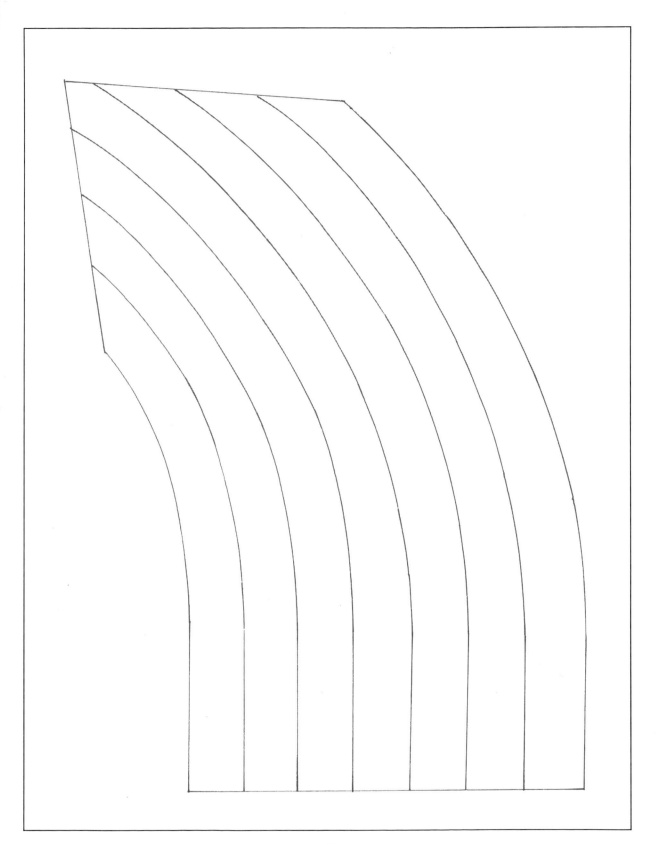

Roll it out to an oblong to fit the top half of the cake, about 10 inches (25 cm) wide and 8 inches (20 cm) high.

Lift the icing on the rolling pin and lay it gently on top of the cake. Press it gently into position and trim neatly at the corners.

Colour the rest of the fondant mid green and apply in the same way. Tuck the icing under the cake and trim. Smooth out any cracks by rubbing the fondant with the dredging mixture.

Now for the rainbow. Trace the rainbow on to a piece of Bakewell paper. Roll out the marzipan to approximately the right shape. It will be quite thick. Lay the design on the icing and cut round with a small sharp knife, dipping the blade in very hot water so that it cuts the marzipan easily. With the design still in place, use the knife to press down on the lines of colour so that the marks come out on the marzipan. You may cut the paper but it doesn't matter.

Take the paper off and start painting. It is easier to start with the red so that the brush is not a dark colour first. The only colour which is not straight from the bottle is indigo: this is blue and black mixed. Do wash the paint brush thoroughly between each colour.

Fuzz the edges of the colours by dampening the brush and running it up and down between the separate colours.

Dab some apricot jam on the cake where the rainbow will go. Lifting the rainbow with a large slice or palette knife, lay it in place. You can wiggle it into the best position and if any jam ends up showing, lift it off with a damp paint brush.

Take some of the remaining marzipan and colour it yellow. Roll it out and cut a small round for the sun. I used a tiny pastry cutter but you could use anything circular about an inch (2.5 cm) or less across. Fix the sun in place with some jam, then cut some very thin sticks of yellow marzipan for the sun's rays and fix on with jam.

The silver balls are raindrops. Lift them with tweezers, dip them lightly into a saucer of jam and push into the blue fondant.

Open one packet of gold coins and brush one side of each coin with jam; fix to the bottom of the rainbow and down the side of the cake. Stick them to the cake and to each other.

The most effective colour to put on the cake board is very dark blue: I bought some paper at the local art shop.

When you put the cake on the table, scatter a few gold coins around the base and if you are going to give each child a bag of coins, pile them up in a heap.

49

Unicorn and Pony

Unicorns are the most mysterious and beautiful of fairytale animals. A friend of mine in the United States told me that Unicorn party cakes were the most sought after by children, mostly romantic girls I think! Perhaps Black Beauty would be more suitable for the boys.

Unicorns only come out at night so I made this one look as if he was galloping across a night sky, with only the moon and stars for light. This beautiful creature prancing up on his hind legs is, as some parents may suspect, inspired by the Lloyds Bank logo. Lloyds display their horse outside every branch and when I was looking for one to copy, I spotted the Lloyds black horse and the bank very kindly agreed to let me use it as a basis for this cake.

The shape and cake can be adapted to any colour combination you wish. I made a palomino rather quickly one morning and he turned out extremely well. A black horse looks marvellous as you can see in the small picture and there are instructions for making him below those for the unicorn.

The cake now takes me an hour to decorate but I think you should allow yourself at least an hour and a half so that you need not rush.

YOU WILL NEED:

Unicorn

CAKE 5 egg Madeira baked in a 9 or 10 inch (22 or 25 cm) round tin

ICING 1 lb (450 gm) fondant icing
8 oz (225 gm) white marzipan

JAM 4 oz (110 gm) warm, sieved apricot jam

COLOURINGS Silver and gold non-toxic poster paint
Dark blue and violet liquid or paste

DECORATIONS Silver balls
Shredded coconut

EXTRAS 12 inch (30 cm) square cake board
White textured paper
Translucent stars (optional)
White candles and holders

Black Beauty

Cake, icing and jam as above

COLOURINGS Black paste
  Blue and green liquid or paste

DECORATIONS Green ball for his eye
  Green sugar to use on grass

EXTRAS Round 12 inch (30 cm) cake board
  Pale green paper
  Pink, blue, yellow and white candles and
  holders

*You will need tweezers and a paint brush
for this cake*

Unicorn

You do not need to freeze the sponge
for this cake recipe, and you can
prepare the decorations while the cake
cools. Trace the stencil of the horse on
to Bakewell paper and cut it out.

Roll out the marzipan and lay the
stencil on it. Cut round it with a small
sharp knife. Paint the Unicorn with
silver paint and put in the freezer or
fridge. Make a crescent moon out of a
little piece of marzipan and paint that
silver too. Make his horn out of a piece
of marzipan 1½ inches (3.5 cm) long and
¼ inch (0.5 cm) wide at the base. Put
these to chill.

Cover the board with the appropriate
paper and paint the candleholders
silver.

When the cake is quite cold, put it
on an upturned plate, brush with jam
and cover with white fondant. Trim
neatly. If you have time, leave the
fondant to dry out, if not start painting.

Use violet and dark blue colours and
wash them over the fondant from side
to side. The night sky is streaky and
mysterious so I painted the cake all
over with dark blue and then started
streaking it with violet. This amount of
colour can make a rather wet surface,
so try and leave it to dry before fixing
the Unicorn in place.

Meanwhile dye the shredded
coconut for his mane and tail with the
gold poster paint.

When the paint is just about dry,
take the Unicorn from the freezer and

peel the paper from the back. Put him on the cake. Smear a little jam on his mane and tail and fix on the golden shredded coconuts with tweezers.

Using tweezers to lift the silver balls and dip them in jam, push the balls into the base of his mane, his hooves and to outline his tail.

Put the cake on the white board and scatter the stars around.

Black Beauty

Make the stencil in the same way.

Dye the marzipan black and then roll out. Cut out the horse and put in the freezer. Dye the shredded coconut by turning it over and over in a small dish of black colouring until it is a uniform black. Spread the coconut on Bakewell paper and leave until needed.

Cover the cake with white fondant and paint the sky pale blue using a medium to small paint brush and a very watery mixture. The effect is best if the blue is patchy. Paint the sides first so that you can practise. Then paint the meadow green in the same way. Load the brush with almost undiluted green colouring to make the line between the sky and grass. Paint this line just away from the blue, leaving about $\frac{1}{8}$ inch (0.25 cm) of white between. It makes it look better but I am not quite certain why.

Sprinkle a few green sugar crystals on the green grass – it doesn't matter if the paint is still wet, it all blends in.

Leave the cake to dry.

Then take the horse out of the freezer and fix him on the cake with jam. Brush a film of jam over his mane and tail. Using tweezers, lay coconut shreds thickly over the jammy bits. Push a green ball into the marzipan for his eye.

Put the black horse cake on the pale green board and push the coloured candles and holders into place round the edge.

Butterflies

One wet summer's day, I went on a marvellous expedition to Syon Park Butterfly Farm. It was steamy warm in the tropical butterfly house and very exotic. Children were swarming around and brightly coloured butterflies were darting from leaf to leaf and resting on our heads and shoulders. The children were as enchanted as I was and that gave me the idea for this easy cake.

I didn't copy specific butterflies, although you could easily do so. I just played about with cake colours, both paste and liquid, using them undiluted and mixing them with gold and silver non-toxic paint or powder to make wonderful metallic effects.

I made the butterfly wings in the photograph different to show what you can do. The red and gold wing is painted on white marzipan and the blue one on fondant.

This cake should take you no longer than two hours in all. Both children and grown-ups loved the butterfly cake which will feed about 12 people.

YOU WILL NEED:

CAKES 2 Victoria sponges made with a 4 egg mixture and baked in 8 inch (20cm) round tins

ICING 1 lb (450 gm) white marzipan or fondant
4 oz/8 oz (110/225 gm) mixture butter icing (p.14)

JAM 4 to 6 oz (110–175 gm) warm, sieved apricot jam

COLOURINGS These are only suggestions:
Silver and gold non-toxic poster paint or colouring powder
Blue, red, pink, green, yellow, orange, violet liquid or watered down paste. The more colours the better

DECORATIONS Coloured balls (dragées)
2 painted cocktail sticks
2 Dolly Mixture jellies – very small

EXTRAS 14 inch (35 cm) square cake board
Pale green wrapping paper
Candles and holders painted silver and gold, and coloured candles

OPTIONAL Small butterfly cutter – it saves time

You will need tweezers and a paint brush for this cake

Use frozen or chilled sponge cakes for
this recipe. It doesn't matter at all if
your sponges dip at one side; position
the lower sides in the middle.

Cut the stencils out in Bakewell
paper. Lay the wing pattern on one
sponge and cut round. Reverse the
stencil and cut a wing from the second
sponge. Cut out the body. Keep the
surplus sponge wrapped in clingfilm.

Body

Attach to body

56

Split all three cakes and fill with two thirds of the butter icing. Mound the icing up at the back of the wings so that the butterfly will point upwards and outwards. Fill the body with enough icing to make it level with the inside wings.

Brush jam on the tops of the wings and body. Roll out the fondant and cut out the wing shapes with the stencil. Fix these in place. Fork the remaining butter icing round the outside of the wings.

Cover the top and sides of the body with some leftover fondant. Trim neatly. Keep the remaining fondant tightly wrapped to use for the little butterflies.

Start painting the cake. I used two different blues and washed the darker over the fondant wing. I mixed silver with the same blue and brushed wide strokes from the inside wing out, adding shading with the other blue. The wing is edged with undiluted silver and I painted short silver strokes on the inside wing by the body. The wingtips are spotted with silver.

Scarlet is the main colour on the marzipan wing, brushed with light and dark pink. The wing is edged and patterned with gold. The body is painted dark blue with gold bands across it, and outlined in a mixture of blue and silver.

Paint the two cocktail sticks blue and stick tiny jellies on the end when they are dry. Push them into the head as antennae. Use two silver balls as eyes, fixing them in place with jam. The icing protects the sponge, so you can store this cake uncovered in a cool dry place overnight. The little butterflies may dry out so make these near the party time or make them the day before and store them in an airtight tin.

They are made from the leftover pieces of sponge. Split the bigger pieces and use a cutter or the stencil to make about eight little butterflies. Brush them with jam. Roll out the fondant, cut out the same number of butterfly shapes and put them on the sponge butterflies. Paint them different colours and when the paint is dry, decorate them with coloured balls.

Cover the cake board with pale green material or paper.

Assemble the cake an hour or two before the party. Put one wing on the board, brush jam on either side of the body and place it by the inside wing. Put the second wing in position. Put the little butterflies around the big one and set the candles at the wing tips.

Racing Car

I made this splendid red Maserati for Tom Pakenham's eighth birthday. I used a model Maserati 250F by Polistil so that I could get the detail more or less right.

My only problem was how to make the wheels and this was solved by a friend, who said that I __must__ use Jaffa cakes in the book somewhere, anywhere . . . so hidden under the silver balls and black marzipan of the wheels are four Jaffa cakes, which worked beautifully for tyres.

Tom has ginger hair but you should colour the driver's hair and eyes to match your child.

This cake will feed about eight children. It will take you between 1½ and 2 hours.

Be careful of the cocktail sticks when children are eating the cake.

YOU WILL NEED:

CAKE 1 large Swiss roll (9 inches/22 cm), frozen

ICING 8 oz (225 gm) fondant icing
8 oz (225 gm) white marzipan

JAM 4 oz (110 gm) warm, sieved apricot jam

COLOURINGS Red and black paste
Yellow, orange, blue, brown paste or liquid
White and silver non-toxic poster paint

DECORATIONS 4 Jaffa cakes
Silver balls (dragées)
1 liquorice pinwheel
4 small yellow jellies (Dolly Mixture size)
Long Matchmakers

EXTRAS 12 or 14 inch (30 or 35 cm) square cake board
Green paper
Candles, candle holders and Ferrero Rocher chocolate hazelnuts

You will need tweezers and a paint brush for this cake

Take the frozen Swiss roll and with a small sharp knife cut the ends as in the diagram. With a grapefruit knife, scoop out the driver's seat. You want to dig down about an inch (2.5 cm). Neaten it off.

Make a sloping cut from the middle along the length of the car to the front to resemble the slope of the bonnet. You only need to slope down about half an inch (1 cm). Brush with jam.

Roll out the red fondant icing and cover the whole car with it. Cut round the hole for the driver's seat, leaving it uncovered but jammy. Put the cake on the board, which you have covered with dull silver paper and black paper. If you transfer the cake later when the fondant has set, it may crack.

Make the wheels from Jaffa cakes. Brush the Jaffa cakes with apricot jam, dye half the marzipan (4 oz/110 gm) black and divide it into 1 oz (30 gm) pieces. Roll out between pieces of Bakewell paper. Lay one little cake in the middle of each piece and pull the sides up and round; push together neatly in the middle. Keep any odd trimmings. Turn over on to the right side. With tweezers, pick up the silver balls, dip them in apricot jam and push them into the wheels to look like spokes: eight spokes of five silver balls each, arranged round one ball in the centre, with three balls on the outside between each spoke. Put the wheels on a piece of Bakewell paper to dry.

Paint three Matchmakers silver and leave to dry. Paint a half width piece of liquorice 3¼ inches (8 cm) long, from the pinwheel, silver and leave to dry.

Colour 2 oz (60 gm) of marzipan bright yellow. Roll out to about ⅛ inch (0.3 cm) thickness. Cut out a strip to make the number for the back. I used a piece 3½ inches (9 cm) long and ¼ inch (0.5 cm) wide to make the figure 8. Form the number, paint the top white with poster paint and leave to dry.

Now make the driver's seat. Cut a rounded square inch for the base and fix in place. Then cut another longer piece about 1 inch by 4 inches (2.5 × 10 cm) to go round the sides and fix in place, joining it at one back corner. Make another rectangle to fit the nose of the car; mine measured 1½ inches (3.5 cm) high by 1¾ inches (4 cm) wide. The top corners should be rounded. Now cut a strip to go round that, just under ½ inch (1 cm) wide and 4½ inches (11 cm) long. Fix all these in place with apricot jam. Lastly make the number plate with a rectangle of yellow marzipan ½ inch (1 cm) high and 1¾ inches (4 cm) wide. Make the letters out of a piece of liquorice from the steering wheel, slit in

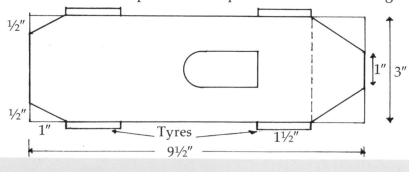

half and cut into short lengths. Stick the letters down with apricot jam. Stick the number plate on the front at the bottom.

Lay the piece of silver liquorice down the centre of the bonnet lengthways.

Push the four yellow jellies into place as lights, two at the rear and one on either side at the front. Now make the radiator from a ¾ inch (2 cm) rounded square of white marzipan, stick it in position above the number plate, between the lights, and then paint it silver and stick silver balls around it. (If there isn't enough space between the lights, just make the radiator a little smaller.)

Now for the driver – the birthday child. You should have 2 oz (60 gm) of white marzipan left. Use 1½ oz (45 gm) for the driver. Take ½ oz (15 gm) and roll most of it into a round head. Form the rest into a small flat piece and stick it on his head like a wig. Paint the face pale pink (watered pink colouring), put on coloured dots for eyes, outlined in silver if you like, to resemble goggles, and make deep pink or red marks for mouth and nose. I used a very wide V for the mouth and a smaller one for the nose. Paint the hair in streaks of the right colours.

Make the body, arms and hands out of the remaining 1 oz (30 gm). Make a fat L-shape for the body and try it in the driver's seat to see whether it fits. Now make arms 1 inch (2.5 cm) long and about ⅓ inch (1 cm) fat. Fix them to the body with apricot jam. Paint the whole of this blue or whatever colour appeals to you. Fix the head to the body with a cocktail stick. Put the driver in his seat. Now take two tiny scraps of marzipan for hands, paint them pink and fix them on to his arms.

Use the remainder of the liquorice pinwheel, which should be the centre and one or two circles of liquorice, for the steering wheel. Fix it in place with a cocktail stick. From the ½ oz (15 gm) of remaining white marzipan, make three ½ inch (1 cm) flat rounds, for the two wing mirrors and the petrol cap. Paint them silver and leave to dry. Take one silver Matchmaker and cut it in two for the mirrors. Stick a silver round on each and push into place on either side of the windscreen. Use the other round for a petrol cap. Push a silver ball in the top and stick it to the car with jam. The other two silver Matchmakers are for the exhaust. Stick them to the side of the car, resting on the left rear tyre.

I used Ferrero Rocher chocolates as bases for the candle holders but you could use anything similar.

Winnie the Pooh

I think this illustrates the most well-known story about Winnie the Pooh. He decides to go after honey which is in a tree guarded by bees. To disguise himself, in the actual story, he rolls himself in mud so that he can pretend to be a small black cloud and deceive the bees. He hangs on to a blue balloon – which he hopes the bees will think is just a round bit of sky – and sets off on his expedition. I decided the cake wouldn't look as attractive if Pooh was muddy, so he is wearing a bright red waistcoat which probably accounts for the eventual failure of the expedition.

The bees are the real hit of this cake. Everyone wants one, so make enough. Benjamin Georget (who tried out this cake on its second run) liked his bee so much he rushed it off to the freezer so that he could keep it for posterity – or the next day at least!

The second big hit is the blue balloon – a <u>real</u> balloon. It would be fun to give each child a blue balloon and a small pot of honey of their own to take home as a party present.

The bees are not difficult but they take some time to make, so allow two hours to decorate this cake. It will feed about 12 people.

YOU WILL NEED:

CAKE 7 inch (18 cm) round Victoria or Madeira sponge made with 3 eggs

ICING 8 oz (225 gm) yellow marzipan 8 oz (225 gm) white marzipan or 8 oz (225 gm) fondant icing

JAM 8 oz (225 gm) warm, sieved apricot jam

COLOURINGS Red, yellow, green paste or liquid

DECORATIONS Long chocolate Matchmakers – about 6 Chocolate vermicelli 1 packet of Peanut Treets 1 small packet chocolate flock 2 currants or 2 chocolate Polka Dots Coloured balls (dragées) Small packet of flaked almonds

EXTRAS 14 inch (35 cm) square cake board Yellow and green paper

Blue string
Blue balloon
Small pot of honey

You will need tweezers for this cake

The cake need not be frozen for this recipe. Level the cake if necessary, and turn upside down on a pudding basin or upturned dinner plate. Brush the cake with a thin layer of apricot jam.

Tint the white marzipan, or fondant, the same shade of green as the green paper. If the green colouring is too bright, add a drop of blue to soften it. Roll out the green icing and cover the cake. Tuck the icing round the bottom of the cake and trim.

Trace the Pooh design on to Bakewell paper. Roll out the yellow marzipan to about ¼ inch (0.5 cm) thick, lay the design on it and cut round the figure. Put it aside on Bakewell paper.

Cut up the Pooh stencil and cut the two ears, the upstretched arm and paw, and left leg from the remaining yellow marzipan. Colour a walnut of the marzipan bright red, and cut out the waistcoat pattern, allowing a little extra on each side. Dab jam on the underside of each of the extra pieces and fix in position on the marzipan Pooh figure.

Use currants or chocolate Polka Dots for his nose and eye. Use two pieces of chocolate vermicelli for his eyebrow and a scrap of red marzipan for his tongue. Stick them all down with apricot jam. With tweezers, dip three silver balls in the jam, and push them into his waistcoat for buttons. Smear a little jam on the soles of his feet and, using a teaspoon, press on a few chocolate vermicelli.

Put Pooh on one side on Bakewell paper to firm up.

Make the bees. It is wise to make at least as many as there are children. Use yellow marzipan or if you have none left over, use some scraps of white coloured yellow. Roll out thinly and then cut into thin strips a generous inch (3 cm) long. Brush them with jam. Hold the Peanut Treet firmly with your left finger and thumb (if you're right-handed), and with your right hand position two strips of marzipan, jam side down, to make the bee's stripes. Put a small jammy blob on one end and, using tweezers, press two coloured balls into it to look like ferocious eyes.

Make the wings out of pieces of flaked almond. Stick them on to the bees with more jam.

Put the bees aside to firm up until you want to assemble the cake.

Before you put the cake together, cover the cake board with yellow paper and cut out circles of green paper to

represent the trees. I used a teacup to draw round for these but you could use any suitable shape, 4 inches (10 cm) or so wide. Stick the circles down overlapping and give them Matchmaker trunks, stuck with jam not glue because they will probably get ripped off and eaten.

Scatter flakes of chocolate or chocolate vermicelli along the bottom of the board to make it look like a forest. Brush the bottom of the board lightly with jam first to make them stick.

You can make up the cake the night before if you like. Stick Pooh on to the cake with a little jam and stick a little pot of honey in the trees. I used Tippex to white out all the words except PURE HONEY, and a small blob of jammy marzipan to stick the pot down.

Put bees all over the trees looking as if they are about to swarm over Pooh. A lazy bee sitting on the honey pot is fun.

Just before the party, blow up the blue balloon and curl Pooh's paw firmly round it. I took one to a friend's house on a windy day and the balloon took off down the street without the cake, so beware of prevailing weather conditions.

Draughtsboard

Caroline Taggart, the editor of this book, suggested this cake. I was reluctant at first because I thought it would be the most dreadful fuss for not much reward. But I was quite wrong – the cake is lovely and you can actually play draughts on it which is great fun.

I spent a long time brooding on how to decorate it simply – trying and rejecting different methods. You will probably want to do it in only two colours, like a real draughts board, but the cake in the photo will give you an idea of the different combinations you can use.

It will probably take you about an hour and a half, all told, and shouldn't make you want to give up half way through.

You could do this cake the day before and leave it in a cool dry place overnight.

This cake will feed about 20 people.

YOU WILL NEED:

CAKE 5 egg Madeira sponge baked in a 9 or 10 inch (22–25 cm) square tin

ICING 1 lb (450 gm) white marzipan
1 lb (450 gm) white fondant
4 oz/8 oz (110/225 gm) mixture lemon butter icing (p. 14)

COLOURINGS 3 colours which complement each other. I used red and blue paste and silver non-toxic poster paint

DECORATIONS Counters such as round white and green peppermints

EXTRAS 14 inch (35 cm) square cake board
Candles and candle holders

OPTIONAL Butter icing for filling made with 6 oz/12 oz (175/335 gm) mixture (p. 14)

This cake does not need to be frozen.

Do not even attempt to ice this on an upturned plate or basin. It is much too big and will break in the middle. Put the cake on a big board. Slit and fill with butter icing if you wish.

Brush with jam and cover the top with white fondant icing.

Trim neatly round the edges.

Use the 4 oz/8 oz (110/225 gm) quantity of butter icing, spiced with at least 1 tbsp of fresh lemon juice and the grated lemon rind, to cover the sides. Put it on with a palette knife and use a fork to make the sides look pretty. Put on the cake board and set on one side.

Knead the marzipan well and roll it

out on Bakewell paper to a depth of just under ¼ inch (0.5 cm), and cut out a piece precisely 8 inches (20 cm) square. I used a set square and this helped. Cut away the extra marzipan and wrap it up for later.

Using a ruler and a small sharp knife, divide each side into eight equal parts by making a notch along each side at 1 inch (2.5 cm) intervals. Dip the knife in boiling water and, using the ruler, join up the notches to make 64 squares. Do not cut through the marzipan but dig the knife in enough to make a distinct groove.

Cut the board into four to make painting it easier. Dip the blade of the knife into boiling water and divide the board into four 2 × 8 inch (5 × 20 cm) strips. Each strip will be two squares wide. Keep the strips in the same order as they were in the square, so that they will join up neatly later.

With a small brush, fill in alternate squares in different colours. You will find that the grooves on each side of the little squares act as barriers and stop the paint spilling over to the next square.

In the photograph I have shown you four different colour combinations. The elegant silver and cream is actually silver paint on one set of squares and natural white marzipan on the other.

Divide the leftover marzipan into four pieces and roll them out with your palm on a piece of Bakewell paper into fat worms just under 9 inches (22 cm) long.

Make a mark in the middle of the big cake and then position the two inside quarters of the board. They should fit together neatly, provided you have kept them in the order of the original square. Then position the outside quarters.

Put the worms round the outside to frame the board.

Set the candles on the corners of the cake and round the sides if you wish.

When the icing is completely dry, set out the peppermints or other sweeties and start playing draughts.

The Red Steam Engine

I made this cake for Jamie Jones' third birthday. He is extremely fond of a red engine in one of his picture books and thought that a birthday cake like that was a very good idea.

Over the years perhaps more people have made steam engine cakes than any other kind, finding that the best way to make them is with a big Swiss roll for the round steam part of the engine and a small Swiss roll for the chimney.

Incidentally a birthday-cake-making grandmother told me she was irritated at having to buy, say, six mini Swiss rolls for a cake recipe and then only using one. These decorations are the objects most prized by children, so put the surplus on a plate and give them to the slow grabbers.

I like this cake very much because it is so jolly and bright. It is very easy to make, so relax and enjoy sticking things in place. It shouldn't take you more than two and a half hours.

It will feed 20 children easily.

YOU WILL NEED:

CAKE 9 inch (22 cm) Swiss roll, with no icing on it, frozen or chilled
1½ chocolate covered mini Swiss rolls
7 to 8 inch (18–20 cm) square Madeira – 3 egg mixture, frozen or chilled

ICING 2 lb (900 gm) yellow marzipan

JAM 4 to 6 oz (110–175 gm) warm, sieved apricot jam

COLOURING Red liquid or paste

DECORATIONS 4 oz (110 gm) Dolly Mixture or similar
1 small tube Smarties
8 Fox's Glacier Mints, the rectangular sort
1 box Chocolate Peppermint Sticks or long Matchmakers for rails
Chocolate vermicelli

EXTRAS 14 inch (35 cm) square cake board
Candles and candle holders, painted silver
Green paper

You will need a paint brush for this cake

It is easier to get the board ready before you start because the cake is quite difficult and heavy to handle when it is finished. Cover the board with green paper and build the cake on the board.

Divide the sponge square in half with a serrated knife.

Leave one half as it is.

Divide the other in two parts – one two thirds of the cake and the other one third, so it looks like this:

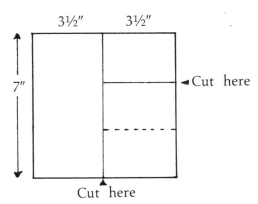

Cut 6 × ½ inch (1.25 cm) slices off the big Swiss roll for the wheels. Brush with jam, dredge with chocolate vermicelli, and fix a small sweet in the centre. Put aside.

Colour 1½ lb (675 gm) of marzipan bright red or, if you prefer, paint the whole engine later.

Roll out the marzipan thinly.

The pieces of sponge are used like this:

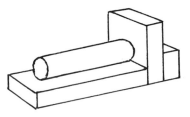

Cover the top and sides of the large flat piece of sponge with marzipan. This is the engine itself. Put on the cake board and brush the back with jam. Cover the top and sides of the larger upright piece of sponge, to make the driving cabin. Cut a piece of marzipan 3½ inches (9 cm) wide and 10½ inches (27 cm) long. Use this to cover the larger sides and the top of the upright piece of sponge, then cover the sides with two pieces about 4½ × 1½ inches (11 × 3.5 cm). Stand it upright and push up against the flat sponge.

Now cover the top and the sides of the coal box at the back of the engine with marzipan. Smear one long side with jam and fix to the driving cabin.

Roll out the marzipan again and cover the top and sides of the Swiss roll – don't bother about the base. From the marzipan, cut two circles with flat bottoms for the front and the back, and fix in place with jam.

Brush the back one with jam and put the Swiss roll in place – it should be an inch (2.5 cm) short of the flat sponge in front but pushed up against the driver's cabin at the back.

Roll out the scraps of marzipan left and cover the outside of the wheels. Set aside.

If you prefer painting the cake, do it now.

Next take the remaining 8 oz (225 gm) yellow marzipan and roll it into long worms about ⅓ inch (1 cm) thick. Use these to outline the different parts of the train. They look good round the bottom front of the engine, round the front of the big Swiss roll, round the driver's cabin and round the coal box so that you can load this up with 'coal'. Use a small paint brush to put jam on the places on the train where you will then fix on the piping.

Fix the one and a half mini Swiss rolls in place with yellow piping and jam.

Use a small piece of marzipan, about 1½ inches (3.5 cm) long, to make a smiling mouth for the front of the train. I used Smarties and a pink sweet from the Dolly Mixture 'coal' to make eyes and nose. Brush a spot of apricot jam on to their backs before putting them in place.

Put a yellow Smartie on the top of the smaller Swiss roll.

Put some jam on the backs of the Glacier Mints, and push them firmly into the marzipan for windows on the driver's cabin. Use two at the front and two at each side. Outline them with slim worms of yellow marzipan.

Brush the top of the coal box with apricot jam and fill with Dolly Mixture 'coal'. Use the yellow jellies and other yellow sweets for lights on the front of the train. Put Dolly Mixture knobs on the doors.

Put the candles in place on the flat bit at the front, and on top of the driver's cabin.

About an hour before the party, stick on the wheels with some apricot jam.

Light the candles and full steam ahead!

Superkid

This cake started life by trying to be the Incredible Hulk, after a special request by Thomas ap Simon. I went to toyshop after toyshop looking for a Hulk to copy and came up with nothing. Was Hulk extinct? And if so, who was Son of Hulk?

There seemed to be the most bewildering array of beastly supermen and I simply couldn't decide which deserved to be immortalised in cake. Something had to be done and I started messing around in the kitchen, standing a big round cake on end to look like a globe and playing with marzipan figures. The idea of Superkid began to take shape. I think he may grow up to be Globe Master.

The actual cake – the globe at night – is simple to decorate and so, surprisingly, is the figure. The knack is in using the globe to support Superkid and in making his limbs separately and leaving them to dry out for two or three days. Marzipan becomes rigid as it dries and is able to support quite a lot of weight.

Superkid is joined up with cocktail sticks so please be very careful when the children start pulling him apart to eat.

The cake will feed about 16 other superkids. If you want to feed more, just increase the quantity of the mixture, but bake it in a similar sized tin. I used a 5 egg Madeira cake baked in a 9 inch (22 cm) tin.

You should decorate the cake the day before the party and make the bits of the figure at least a day earlier.

We used dry ice, available from distillers, to create the swirling mist effect. You could recreate this at home, but it is quite a performance.

YOU WILL NEED:

CAKE 9 inch (22 cm) round Madeira made with 4 or 5 egg mixture (not food processor recipe – it has to stand up)

ICING 1 lb (450 gm) fondant
1 lb (450 gm) marzipan

JAM 4 oz (110 gm) warm, sieved apricot jam

SUPERKID

COLOURINGS Dark blue liquid
   Red paste preferably
   Light blue paste preferably
   Silver non-toxic poster paint
   Yellow liquid
DECORATIONS Small tube of Smarties
   Coloured balls
   Candles and holders
EXTRAS Cocktail sticks
   10 inch (25 cm) square or round cake
   board
   Wrapping paper

You will need tweezers and small paint brushes for this cake.

The cake does not have to be frozen for this recipe.

Slice an arc about 4 inches (10 cm) long off the cake so that it will stand up firmly. Then lay flat. Brush the cake with jam. Roll out the fondant and cover the cake with it, except for the flat side. Trim round the sides.

Paint the cake dark blue with liquid colouring and set aside to dry. Save the leftover fondant to make the cloak.

Now for the Superkid.

He is made up of the following quantities of marzipan:

Head: 2 oz (55 gm) – ½ oz (15 gm) for hair, 1½ oz (40 gm) for face

Chest: 4½ oz (125 gm)

Lower body: 2 oz (55 gm)

Legs/Boots: 3 oz (80 gm) split in to 1½ oz (40 gm) per leg

Arms: 1½ oz (40 gm) split into ¾ oz (20 gm) per arm

Swirlies for his shoulder pads: 1 oz (30 gm) each

Breastplate: ½ oz (15 gm)

Put all the bits on Bakewell paper as you make them. Start with his head. Roll the 1½ oz (40 gm) ball for his face. Paint it pale pink at the front. Then roll worms from ½ oz (15 gm) marzipan for his hair. Fix them on with jam. Paint them yellow. Push green balls into his face for eyes, a pink one for his nose and paint on a red mouth.

His chest is a cube of marzipan, narrowed at the waist and widened at the shoulders. My cube before I shaped it measured about 1¾ inches (4 cm) all round. Paint this bright red.

His lower body is a rectangular block about 1¾ inches (4 cm) wide and 1 inch (2.5 cm) deep and high, narrowed at the top a little and correspondingly wider at the thighs. I ran a knitting needle from front to back in the middle to indicate the tops of his two legs. His legs are made out of fat L-shaped sausages of marzipan. They are just under 2 inches (5 cm) tall and the boots are about 1¾ inches (4 cm) long. Stick a cocktail stick through his boots from top to bottom to encourage them to stay upright. Paint them silver.

Make his arms by rolling out two

thick sausages of marzipan, rather wider at the shoulders, just under 2 inches (5 cm) long. Paint these red.

When the red paint on his arms is dry, use scraps of marzipan to make worms and wind these round his right arm, stuck on with jam, to look like an elaborate arm band. Stud this with metallic balls in coloured bands, stuck on with more jam.

Make his breastplate with a round thick piece of marzipan about 1½ inches (3.5 cm) in diameter. Paint this silver and stick a red Smartie in the middle with jam. Stick this on to his upper body with jam and allow it to set lying down. These pieces should dry for at least one day, preferably two to three.

Use the leftover marzipan to cut out a simple spaceship from the stencil on page 124. Paint this silver and leave to dry. When the paint is dry, glue it to the globe cake with jam. Stud silver balls into the cake to spell out SUPERKID. Outline the cake with silver balls. Cover the cake board with dark blue paper.

Assemble the cake on the day of the party, a couple of hours beforehand. Stand the cake on the board. Put the silver boots on the board just in front of the cake and then position Superkid's

lower body on top of them, pushing it firmly into the cocktail sticks. Stick three cocktail sticks into this. Then put his chest, complete with breastplate, on top, wedging it on to the cocktail sticks.

Attach his head to the top with another cocktail stick. Put a cocktail stick at right angles to his shoulder and drive the rest through his right arm.

Let his left arm, which will be covered by the cloak, hang down his side, secured by another cocktail stick. Colour the fondant you have left over from the globe cake bright blue. Roll it out and make a big wedge shape about 2 inches (5 cm) across the top, 4 inches (10 cm) at the bottom and 5 to 6 inches (12.5–15 cm) long.

Brush jam down Superkid's left side and fix the cloak round his neck and swirling down his side. Fondant is very easy to fold so you can be quite adventurous.

Make a fat worm out of the leftover fondant and put it round his neck. Attach it to his cloak on his left shoulder.

Put a candle and holder in his right hand and Superkid is off to conquer the universe.

Gold and Silver Drum

I made this cake for one of my favourite children, Max Webster. Max is three and he bounces. When I came through the front door with the cake (which he wasn't expecting), he was so excited that he bounced up and down for about five minutes telling me all the time what a lovely cake it was and how excited he was; every other sentence he got a little muddled – the cake was excited and Max was lovely. Anyway it was a great success: he ate the drumsticks before the other guests arrived!

This is one of the most colourful cakes in the book and is very easy but takes patience. I rejected the idea of making separate triangles of gold and silver fondant for the sides because it is more complicated. However, painting the white fondant silver and gold and separating the triangles with silver ball bearings is very simple.

It is a good idea to make enough drumsticks to give one to each child. Arrange them around the bottom of the cake.

The cake will take about two to three hours and feed 16 to 20 children. It will keep well for several days.

This cake is illustrated at the front of the book.

YOU WILL NEED:

CAKE 4 egg Madeira baked in round 8 or 9 inch (20 or 22 cm) tin

ICING 1½ lb (675 gm) white marzipan
8 oz (225 gm) white fondant

JAM 4 oz (110 gm) warm, sieved apricot jam

COLOURINGS Gold and silver non-toxic poster paint or powder cake colouring
Red paste (liquid if necessary)

DECORATIONS Silver balls
Smarties
Jelly diamonds
Ferrero Rocher chocolate hazelnuts
Candy sticks or long Matchmakers

EXTRAS 12 inch (30 cm) round cake board
Blue paper
Candles and holders painted gold and silver

You will need tweezers and a paint brush for this cake

GOLD AND SILVER DRUM

Turn the levelled cake upside down so that you are using the flat surface.

Put the cake on an upturned basin or plate and brush it all over with jam.

Cover the top of the cake with fondant and the sides with marzipan. Use about 12 oz (335 gm) marzipan and roll it out in a strip the measurements of the depth and circumference of the cake. Do the sides first and the top second, or the soft fondant will look bashed up by the time you finish with the sides.

Dye the rest of the white marzipan bright red and roll it out into a fat worm to go round the top and bottom of the drum. It is important that it is firm, so use paste or paint the marzipan red later.

Don't faint, but you will need about 50 inches (125 cm) of this red strip or worm to go round the top and bottom of the cake. When you join the marzipan pieces, don't put the ends on top of each other because that makes a big lump. Cut them neatly so that the ends just touch.

Stick the marzipan on to the cake with jam and leave to set for an hour or so.

Now use the circumference of the cake, which you measured for the red strips. Mine was 25½ inches (64 cm).

Divide it by eight, which makes 3¼ inches (8 cm). This is the width of the base of each triangle. Mark the cake at the bottom with silver balls, 3¼ inches (8 cm) apart. Then take a line vertically from one ball and go up at right angles to the bottom of the cake. Now move sideways by half the width of the base measurement, i.e. just under 1¾ inches (4 cm) on my cake. Put a marker there, and repeat all round the top at intervals of 3¼ inches (8 cm). With your paint brush, mark a thin silver line from the top to the bottom markers all round so that the triangles are clearly outlined. Then fill in the ones which point downwards with gold paint and the ones which point upwards with silver. Using tweezers, dip the silver balls in a shallow puddle of apricot jam and put them down the lines of the triangles as you can see in the photograph. Arrange Smarties all round the top edge. Stick jelly diamonds on the painted triangles with a little jam.

Make the drumsticks by pushing the candy sticks into the foil-wrapped hazelnuts. If you are using long Matchmakers, make a hole in the chocolate hazelnuts first with a skewer or the Matchmakers will break.

Put candles on top of the cake.

Noah's Ark

Alexandra and Ross Stacey, aged 4 and 2, live in Somerset surrounded by animals of all kinds. They are my niece and nephew and I made this cake for them. Lions and tigers have not yet invaded peaceful Chard but as the children have an amazing collection of other beasts, birds and insects, I thought they would appreciate ladybirds nudging tigers on the expedition and butterflies climbing up the mountain to join the bees on the roof of the ark.

The basic ark is very easy to make and should not take longer than an hour and a half. Once you have done that, you can spend as little or as long a time as you like on the animals. If you are pushed for time, make the ark, set it on the sea and raid your nearest good sweetshop and bakery for every animal, bird and insect in sight.

There are lots of different sorts, chocolate, foil-wrapped, marzipan, etc and it shouldn't be difficult to collect enough. And of course, you can always mix bought and homemade as I did for the photograph.

If you find one particularly endearing breed, or if you don't have much choice, create an alternative ark where the animals went in three by three or whatever suits you.

If you decide to make all the animals, you should allow at least four hours to do the whole cake. I left my ark in the kitchen for 24 hours and neither ark nor animals came to any harm. You could easily make the entire cake the day before and leave it in a cool dry place. Alternatively, you could begin making the animals days or weeks earlier and store them in the fridge or a biscuit tin.

The cake will feed 12 to 16 children.

YOU WILL NEED:

For the ark and the sea

CAKE 3 egg Victoria sponge made in a 2 pint (1.1 litre) pudding basin

2 egg Victoria sponge made in an 8 inch (20 cm) sandwich tin with straight sides – frozen or chilled

ICING 1 lb (450 gm) white marzipan
1½/3 oz (45/85 gm) quantity of chocolate butter icing (p. 14)

JAM 4 oz (110 gm) warm, sieved apricot jam

COLOURINGS Red and blue, preferably paste

CARAMEL 8 oz (225 gm) granulated sugar, 8 fl oz (225 ml) water

DECORATIONS 1 packet Cadbury's Chocolate Buttons
Hundreds and thousands
A few Liquorice Allsorts

EXTRAS 14 inch (35 cm) round cake board
Green paper or felt
Silver foil
Cocktail sticks

It is easier to make the ark if the round sponge is frozen or chilled.

First make the caramel by heating the sugar and water together (p. 15). Mix in some blue to make it a good bright sea colour and leave on a moderate heat for about 10 minutes. It will probably take nearer 20 minutes but you should keep an eye on it after 10.

Cover the round cake board with green paper or felt and stick down firmly. Put a blob of jam in the middle and fix on a circle of silver foil just less than the size of the board. Crinkle up the edges about 1½ inches (3.5 cm) from the outside of the board to form a caramel barrier. The blue caramel is the sea surrounding the green mountain. The animals are walking round the edge of the board and they need something firm to walk on – they fall over on caramel.

When the caramel is cooked, pour it round the barrier first, then towards the centre of the board. Try and leave a hole in the middle where the green pudding basin cake will be – this is not absolutely necessary, so if you are flustered with hot caramel just slosh the whole lot on and swirl it out towards the barrier.

Brush the pudding basin cake with jam and cover with green marzipan. The green colour need not be perfectly mixed in to the icing – it looks more realistic if it is a bit blotchy. Keep the trimmings for later, wrapped in clingfilm.

When the caramel is set (about half an hour), put the mountain on it.

Now take your cold round sponge cake and, using the stencils, cut it into three shapes, the roof, the house, and the main boat.

Brush the top of the main boat with jam and cover it with 3 oz (85 gm) white marzipan rolled out thickly. Trim neatly, brush with jam and dredge

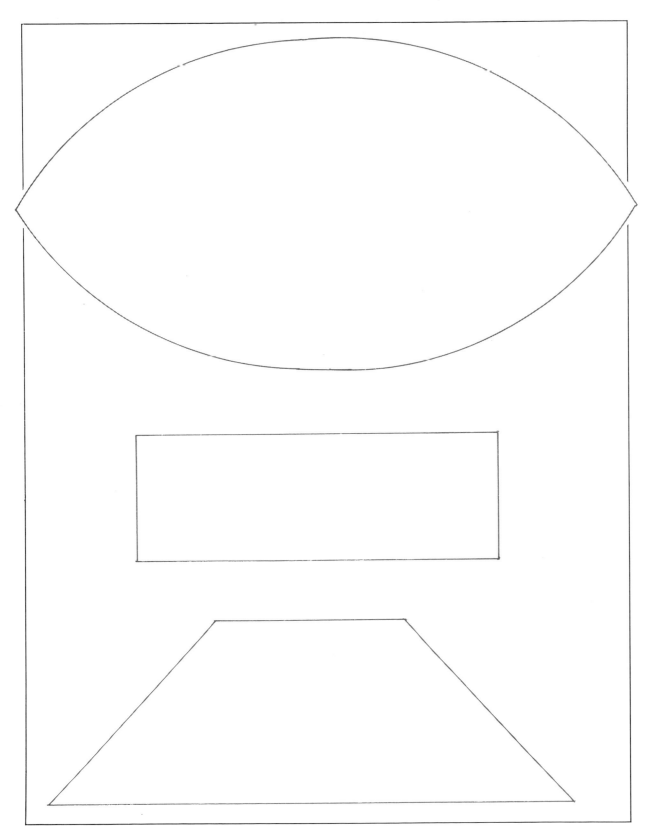

with hundreds and thousands.

Now cover the sides of the boat with half the chocolate icing, forked to look like planks of wood.

Set the boat on the mountain.

The cube of sponge is the house. Paint with jam and cover with bright red marzipan. I used the trimmings from the deck and some more white marzipan adding up to about 4 oz (110 gm). (You will have some over; save this for the ladybirds.)

The easiest way to cover the cube of sponge is to jam the top and sides, roll the marzipan out thinly and plonk it over the top, press it against the sides and just trim the surplus from the corners, pressing any raw edges together. (This is much quicker and easier than it sounds.) Brush the top with jam.

Cover the curved piece of sponge for the roof with the rest of the chocolate icing, set in place and press Chocolate Buttons all over.

Put all this aside – in a cool place because of the chocolate icing and buttons – and decide which animals you fancy.

Animals

The amount of icing is enough for a pair of each animal. *Please be careful with the cocktail sticks when children start picking up the animals. Remove the sticks first.*

Noah

Trimmings of white marzipan adding up to 3 oz (85 gm).
Smartie
Colouring: blue, yellow, pink, brown and red
Cocktail stick

Colour 1½ oz (45 gm) bright blue for his body. Form most of it into a cone 1½ inches (3.5 cm) high and the same width at the base. Pull off 2 tiny worms to use for his arms and fix them on with jam. Roll another ½ oz (15 gm) into his head and paint with pink skin, brown hair, beard and moustache, red nose, mouth and cheeks. Attach his head to his body with a cocktail stick – you will stick the other end of the cocktail stick into the deck so don't cut it off.

Colour the rest of the marzipan yellow and roll it out for his cloak. Cut it out into a semicircle with a radius of 1½ inches (3.5 cm), leaving a small semicircle for the neck. Paint a little jam on his shoulders and fix the cloak on. Drape it so that it looks natural and fold one of the front bits back. Use trimmings of marzipan to make a wide strip to fold over his head as a hood, and fix with jam. Fix a jammy Smartie under his chin to represent his cloak fastening. Put Noah on the deck in front of the ark, pushing the cocktail stick into the deck to fix him in place. You may find you have to move the house part of the ark back a fraction to make room, and make sure it all balances.

Ladybirds

About 2 oz (55 gm) leftover red marzipan (a bit more or less is fine)
16 Chocolate Polka Dots or currants

Roll the marzipan into two balls. Put them on a board and flatten the bases. Brush the Polka Dots with a little jam and push in to look like spots and eyes. I used 6 plain Polka Dots per ladybird for the spots, pushed in pointed side down, and 2 milk Chocolate Polka Dots each for eyes, pushed in the other way round.

Butterflies

Leftover green marzipan (about 1 oz/30 gm)
Paint, paint brush and decorations

Use the leftover green marzipan and the stencil on page 56. Paint and decorate them colourfully. I painted the wings silver and stuck on coloured balls, sugar balls and Smarties.

Leave them to dry with their wings propped up so that they look as if they are flying. When they are stiff and dry, fix them in place with jam.

Bees

Use scraps of marzipan, flaked almonds, coloured balls and Peanut Treets to make the bees detailed on page 63.

Baby Chicks (or ducklings)

3 oz (85 gm) yellow marzipan
4 coloured balls for eyes

These little birds are a bit confused about their identity. They were meant to be chicks but look more like ducks. Anyway they are very sweet and very easy. Take nearly 1½ oz (45 gm) of yellow marzipan and roll 1 oz (30 gm) into a ball. Pull one side out to form a tail. Make 2 flat tiny blobs for feet and put one either side. Roll nearly all the rest into another ball for the head and stick on with jam. Use a tiny worm of marzipan for a beak. Paint beak and feet orange and stick in silver or coloured balls for eyes.

Rabbits

4 oz (110 gm) marzipan
Brown paste or paint
4 balls for eyes

Divide the marzipan in two. If you have chocolate brown paste colouring, colour the icing now. If you have liquid, paint the rabbits later.

Use just over 1 oz (30 gm) to make one rabbit's body. Roll it into a ball and set on the board. Make a smaller ball out of about ⅓ oz (10 gm) for his head and use the rest to make a big tail and four thick worms about ⅓ to ½ inch (about 1 cm) long for feet. Stick these on with jam, but secure the head to the body with half a cocktail stick.

Lions and Tigers

The idea for these came from Rosemary Wadey's book on Cake Making and Decorations. I have adapted them from her basic idea with a few suggestions of my own.

Use 8 to 10 oz (225–285 gm) yellow marzipan. Divide it into four roughly equal pieces. You need orange and black colouring for the tigers, gold or orange for the lions, and coloured balls for their eyes.

Tigers

Use ½ oz (15 gm) for the tail and head, and the rest for the body. Form this into a fat rectangle about 2½ inches (6 cm) or more long. Now bend up 1 inch (2.5 cm) at either end at right angles.

With a small sharp knife slit the two ends to form four legs. Don't slit too far or the legs will not support the body. Turn it up the other way and pull the legs outwards. Pull a thick fat tail out of the ½ oz (15 gm) left and stick on with jam. Roll the rest into a ball, pull out two little ears and point them forwards. Use half a cocktail stick to attach the head to the body. Push in two green balls for eyes. Paint the whole tiger orange, leave to dry, then paint on black tiger stripes. Leave to dry overnight or longer.

Lions

Lions are basically the same design. Use ¾ oz (22 gm) for the lion's head, mane and tail and the rest for the body. The mane is thin worms of marzipan stuck on with jam. A lion's tail is thinner and shorter than a tiger's and it has a bobble at the end: make it out of a slightly longer worm than the mane. Paint only his feet, mouth and mane ends with gold or orange. Stick in green or gold balls for eyes.

Extra Animals

The lovely silver fish are on sale in lots of chocolate shops and so are the chocolate snails, which come in a box or loose with chocolate seahorses, and various chocolate shellfish.

The more animals you pile on, the more fun it is, so you could add some cut-out animals from the stencils on page 124, walking round the mountain.

Guardsman

When I drew the prototype
for the guardsman, he looked
most peculiar, rather like
Incredible Hulk in fancy dress.

A friend who is a proper
artist had to come and rescue
me and he produced this
splendid looking fellow. We
know he is a 'good'
Guardsman, by the way,
because of the medal on his
chest. He will feed 12 to 16
guests.

YOU WILL NEED:

CAKE 7 inch (18 cm) square Victoria
   sponge, made from 3 or 4 egg mixture
ICING 12 oz (335 gm) fondant (if bought,
   two 8 oz (225 gm) blocks)
   8 oz (225 gm) white marzipan
JAM 6 oz (175 gm) warm, sieved apricot
   jam
COLOURINGS Red, navy blue, chocolate
   brown, black paste if possible
   Yellow, green, pink liquid or paste
   Silver, gold, white non-toxic poster
   paint
DECORATIONS Chocolate vermicelli
   A raisin, 2 currants or
   2 Chocolate Polka Dots
   Box of Smarties
   Cadbury's Chocolate Buttons

Cadbury's Chocolate Fingers
Silver and coloured balls (dragées)
Box of Chocolate Peppermint Sticks or
long Matchmakers

*You will need tweezers and a paint brush
for this cake*
This cake should be kept in the fridge

Trace the Guardsman design on to
Bakewell paper.

Roll out the marzipan to about ¼
inch (0.5 cm) thick, lay the design on
it and cut round, dipping the blade of
a small sharp knife in boiling water so
that it cuts easily. Put the figure on
one side to dry on Bakewell paper.

Cut up the paper design into these
pieces: bearskin, face, collar, tunic,
hands, trousers and feet. Cut up the
tunic pattern to make a stencil for his
belt only after you have cut out his
tunic in marzipan.

Take a walnut-sized piece of
marzipan (about ¾ oz/22 gm) and roll it
out thickly. Use this for the bearskin.
Cut round the shape and then paint it
chocolate brown. If you prefer, you
could dye it before cutting it out.
Leave the brown marzipan to dry a
little and then dab it with jam and
push chocolate vermicelli thickly into
it to resemble the bear's fur. Take a tiny
piece of marzipan for his plume, paint
it yellow and fix it on with a dab of jam.
Brush the main figure with a little jam

and fix the bearskin firmly in place. Push the edges down the sides of the main figure so that the white marzipan doesn't show. A few more chocolate vermicelli pushed round the edge help with this too.

Take a small half of the leftover marzipan and colour it bright red. Roll it out, lay the design for the tunic on it and cut out, being sure to leave a little extra on the outside edges – so that you can press the tunic down the side of the base figure. Fix on with jam.

Now take a small piece of marzipan, about ½ inch (1 cm) square, and make his face. Push this into position under the bearskin and paint pink. Push in two currants or half-raisins for eyes, nearly disappearing under his bearskin, and a red marzipan mouth.

Mould two hands out of white marzipan, fix them in place with jam and paint them really white with poster paint.

Cut his belt out, fix it on with jam and then neatly paint it white.

Make his chinstrap with a tiny strip of marzipan, twisted and painted silver. Dab it with jam and use tweezers to put it in place. Make his belt buckle with a strip of marzipan, formed into a square, painted yellow and then finished off with gold paint. Make stripes on his cuffs in the same way, and

stick them on with a tiny dab of jam.

I made his medal green but you can make it any colour you like – it just needs to look impressive. This one is a circle of marzipan about ⅓ inch (1 cm) wide, with a green ball in the middle and a triangle on top about the same size as the circle.

Push silver balls down his front for buttons. Use tweezers to pick them up, dip them in jam and then push them into his tunic.

Colour the rest of the white marzipan dark blue and use for his collar and trousers. Cut out the trousers with a little extra width on the outside edges and fix on with jam. Cut out his collar neatly and fix in place. Trim his trousers with strips of red marzipan down the outsides, fixed with jam, and his collar with two coloured balls.

His boots are two rounds of blue marzipan stuck on to his trousers and then painted with black colouring.

Leave the whole figure to dry; if you are in a hurry, put it in the freezer or the fridge.

Take the square sponge and cut into two rectangles one 7 inches by 4 inches (18 × 10 cm) and one 7 inches by 3 inches (18 × 8 cm). Set the big one on a cake board with the long side running north to south. Lay the smaller one

longways across it so that the two cakes make an upside down L shape with a straight left edge and an overlapping square 3 inches by 3 inches (8 × 8 cm) on the top right. Cut off the square. Glue the other two pieces together with jam to form a tall rectangle 10 inches by 4 inches (30 × 10 cm).

Now take the leftover square, cut diagonally into two triangles and cut one of the triangles in two again. Put the larger triangle, pointed side up, across the top of the rectangle to form the gable of the sentry box, and the shorter ones at right angles to the sides to make the eaves. Glue them all in place with jam.

Cover the whole of the cake with jam.

Roll out the white fondant thickly to a rectangle the size of the cake top. Lay in place and trim to size using a ruler or straight edge and small sharp knife. You will have some fondant left over from this operation but the sentry box is such an odd shape you will never cover it in one piece unless you start off with this amount. Don't worry if it breaks or won't fit. Join as neatly as possible and smooth the surface of the fondant with some icing sugar and cornflour from the dredger.

Now apply the chocolate butter icing to the sides. Put it on thickly with a palette or table knife. Stick the chocolate buttons on to the roof and the chocolate fingers down the sides and bottom.

By now the figure of the Guardsman should have firmed up a bit. Brush the centre of the sentry box with a few blobs of jam to anchor him. Peel him off the Bakewell paper backing and fix in place.

Glue the silver or gold paper on to the cake board and put the cake on the board.

Using Chocolate Peppermint Sticks or Matchmakers, make railings and glue them on to the board with jam. Top the upright railings with red and yellow Smarties.

I scattered the bottom of the cake board with gold dust to look grand; you could use some more chocolate vermicelli or anything like that. The candles are blue magic candles stuck into ordinary holders which have a big blob of red marzipan stuck on top of them, and silver balls around the base of the candles.

To display the Guardsman at his best, prop up the back of the cake board with a saucer. The cake should not slip and it does look splendid.

Chocolate Castle

The local estate agent suggested this subject to me. Men are usually rather uninterested in party cakes and I was surprised to find him so forthcoming. It turned out that his six-year-old son Richard had demanded a proper castle cake for his party with towers and a moat and everything, and that is why his father was so well informed.

This cake is a very simple basic idea, just two square cakes, one cut and put on top of the other, but the interest comes from heavy use of Cadbury's 'accessories' in the form of Crunchies, Chocolate Buttons, Chocolate Flakes, Wispas and my long time favourite Chocolate Fudge Bars.

The towers are edible ice cream tubs turned upside down and coated with chocolate. I used the cornets called 'sundae cups' but if you can't find these in your local store, the traditional cone-shaped cornets would do quite well.

This cake feeds a lot of children – in fact it is almost a party tea in itself so you don't have to provide too much other food. It is certainly enough for sixteen children. Apart from the jelly moat and the chocolate drawbridge, you could assemble this cake the night before, and it shouldn't take you more than an hour and a half. Leave it in a cold place overnight because of the chocolate.

YOU WILL NEED:

CAKE 7 or 8 inch (17 or 20 cm) square sponge cake made with a 4 egg mixture The same size cake made with a 2 egg mixture (I used chocolate sponges)

ICING Chocolate butter icing made with 10 oz (285 gm) icing sugar, 6 oz (175 gm) soft butter, 6 oz (175 gm) chocolate powder melted in 3 tbsp (60 ml) coffee (or water or orange juice) (p. 14)

JAM 2 oz (55 gm) warm, sieved apricot jam

DECORATIONS 4 'sundae' cornets coated in 2 oz (55 gm) block chocolate melted in 2 tbsp (40 ml) coffee or water
2 Crunchies
2 Cadbury's Chocolate Flakes (3 inch/ 7.5 cm size)

4 oz (110 gm) Cadbury's Chocolate Buttons
2 Wispa bars
4 Cadbury's Fudge Bars (4 inch/10 cm size)
8 oz (225 gm) large nuts or 2½ lb (generous 1 kg) brightly coloured jellies
2 pints (1.1 litre) of blue jelly made from 2 pints (1.1 litre) water and 2 oz (55 gm) gelatine, blue colouring and peppermint essence to flavour it

EXTRAS 14 inch (35 cm) square cake board
Candles and holders

FLAG POLE Piece of crêpe paper and something like a piece of seaside rock for the pole – a pencil or a candy stick will do fine

OPTIONAL Toy soldiers

You will need tweezers and a skewer for this cake

The cakes can be frozen or unfrozen, it doesn't matter. Make the jelly and put to set. When it is set, chop up with a sharp knife and store in the fridge until needed.

Holding the cornets with tweezers, dip them in the melted chocolate and coffee mixture. The coffee really doesn't taste, it just makes the chocolate more chocolatey, but if you prefer, use water or orange juice. Put the cornets to drip dry on a cake rack or grill.

Cover the bigger cake with about half the chocolate butter icing and put on the cake board.

Cut the other cake in half and use a 1½ inch (3.5 cm) cutter to make eight rounds. Use these to make the four towers. This is a nice messy job – and you need to lick the icing off your fingers quite a lot. Push a skewer through a round of sponge, put some butter icing on top, then add another round of sponge, making sure that the height is the same all round. Holding the skewer firmly, coat the sides of the tower with more icing. When this is done, slide the tower off the skewer and put it in place at a corner of the base. Repeat with the other three towers. When the cornets are dry, put these on top.

Now make the walls and ramparts of the castle with the other half of the cake. Cut it into four rectangles about 3½ inches (8 cm) by 1½ inches (3.5 cm). Cover three of the four rectangles of cake with chocolate icing on tops and sides (the remaining piece is spare). Set them on the cake base. Push the towers well up against these walls. Now add three Fudge bars, each cut up in to three pieces, on the top of each wall to look like battlements.

Make the portcullis with two Crunchie and one Fudge bar as shown in the photograph.

CHOCOLATE CASTLE

Now decorate the castle with Cadbury's Chocolate Buttons, which children always love, pushed into the chocolate icing.

I decided that the inside of the castle needed some interesting flooring so I scattered hundreds and thousands thickly over it – you could use something else like popcorn, if you prefer.

Keep this cake in a cool place until about an hour before the party. Now finish off by putting the large nuts or coloured jellies round the edge of the board. Anchor them by smearing the board with apricot jam first. Put the two Flakes across as the drawbridge, resting on two Wispa bars. Push candles into the towers and the flag pole in to the top of the castle. Make a flag saying 'Richard's Castle' – or whatever the name of the birthday child is – and tape it on to the flag pole.

When it is nearly time to eat the cake, spread the blue jelly around to fill the moat. You could put some toy soldiers in the castle yard and on the drawbridge as an optional extra: we borrowed ours from Pollocks Toy Museums.

Computer

Polly Drew is seven and her father is a computer genius so I thought that she should have a computer cake for her birthday.

The biggest labour-saving device on this cake is to use Cadbury's Chocolate Buttons for keys. If you felt really energetic, you could pipe letters or numbers on them, but I don't think it is necessary. Children like Chocolate Buttons and in any case they are usually busy gasping at the screen. The impact of the metallic balls on the vertical black screen is stunning. The letters look as if they are lit up.

The size of tins used for the cake needs some explanation. The computer is made up of two sponge cakes: a big square one at the back and a rectangular one at the base, the long side of which should be about the same size as the base of the square cake.

Provided you stick to this scheme, the actual size of tins you use does not matter, except that it would be difficult to decorate if the big cake was less than 9 inches (22 cm) square.

I used a 10 inch (25 cm) square tin with a 5 egg Madeira mixture for the big cake, and a 3 egg mixture in a rectangular roasting tin for the keyboard cake which measured $6\frac{1}{2} \times 12$ inches (16 $\times$ 30 cm). To make the keyboard cake fit the screen cake, I sliced off 2 inches (5 cm), making it $6\frac{1}{2} \times 10$ inches (16 $\times$ 25 cm). You could substitute an 8 inch (20 cm) square tin for the keyboard cake. You would have to cut a slice 2 $\times$ 8 inches (5 $\times$ 20 cm) off one side, cut it down to 2 $\times$ 6 inches (5 $\times$ 15 cm) and add that to the cake to make the keyboard the right shape.

The cake will take you two to three hours to ice and decorate and will feed at least 30 people. But the icing needs to set, so it's best to start the day before. Do not use the food processor recipe – it is not firm enough to stand up.

NOT TO BE RUSHED

YOU WILL NEED:

CAKE 5 egg Madeira sponge baked in 9 to 10 inch (22.5–25 cm) square tin frozen or chilled
3 egg Madeira sponge baked in an 8 inch (20 cm) square tin or other (see above)

ICING 2½ lb (1.1 kg) white fondant
8 oz (225 gm) white marzipan

JAM 4 oz (110 gm) warm, sieved apricot jam

COLOURINGS Black liquid or paste
Silver non-toxic paint

DECORATIONS Large packet of Cadbury's Chocolate Buttons
Small bar of milk or plain chocolate
2 Cadbury's Fudge Bars
Fruit pastilles, jellies or Liquorice Allsorts
Coloured balls (dragées)
Small quantity of Dolly Mixture, say 4 oz (110 gm)

EXTRAS 14 inch (35 cm) square cake board
Coloured paper
Candles and holders

OPTIONAL 2 pieces of liquorice painted silver
2 pink sugar mice

You will need tweezers and a paint brush for this cake

Don't try to ice these cakes on upturned plates, they are too big. Put them on a flat board or rack. Make the screen first.

Use the cake rounded side up – it balances and looks better like that.

Brush the whole cake with jam.

Knead together 1½ lb (675 gm) of fondant and roll out to a big square large enough to cover the whole cake, i.e. about 13 × 13 inches (33 × 33 cm).

Lift the icing with a rolling pin and put it on the cake. Don't worry if the icing breaks on the way, keep cool and carry on – you can patch it and the screen will probably hide any joins.

Trim neatly and put on one side.

Now colour the marzipan black – you don't need a ferocious black, almost deep charcoal. Use either liquid black or paste.

Roll out the marzipan between sheets of Bakewell paper so you get a nice shiny screen and trim it to a rectangle about 7 × 6 inches (17 × 15 cm). Work out where you are going to put it and brush the shape in jam on the big cake. Lay the marzipan on it and set aside to firm.

Use the remaining marzipan to make worms to outline the screen. They should be about ⅓ inch (just under 1 cm) wide and just longer than the length of each side. Fix them in place with jam and join neatly at the corners.

Take a small paint brush and paint the worms silver.

Now stick in the small sweets, jellies, Dolly Mixture etc as knobs on the right of the screen.

The longest bit is next. Using tweezers and a shallow saucer of jam, dip the balls in jam and fix them in place on the black marzipan screen to make the birthday greeting. I made Polly's name bigger than the Happy Birthday so it would stand out. When you have finished this, lay the cake in a cool dry place to set. This is important, so try and allow a few hours and preferably overnight.

The keyboard is very easy. Trim the cake to size. If the cake slopes at all, let it slope up at the back – this is what real keyboards do.

Knead together 1 lb (450 gm) fondant and any trimmings from the other cake. Roll out thickly to a rectangle big enough to cover the keyboard cake, probably 13 × 9 inches (33 × 22 cm).

Brush the cake, top and sides, with jam and lift the fondant into place with a rolling pin. Trim the fondant neatly, especially at the front.

Now have fun with the Chocolate Buttons. I used 3 rows of 12 buttons and one row of 13 for the keys in the middle – 12, 13, 12, 12; two Chocolate Fudge Bars for the space bars at the bottom and squares of block chocolate for the keys at the sides. In the corners, I put pink and green Smarties and Dolly Mixture but the colours and exact choice of sweetie is up to you.

Put the keyboard cake on the covered board – royal blue paper looks good. Just before the party, stand the screen cake upright at the back. I didn't cover this one at the back but if you felt strongly that you wanted to, you could fork a 4 oz/8 oz (110/225 gm) mixture of butter icing on to it. Put the appropriate number of candles on the cake.

Despite my boyfriend's forebodings, the screen cake remained staunchly in place while it was carried from pillar to post, but a car ride was too much. Yours should not need any propping up, but if by chance it seems in danger of toppling, some small heavy object at the back should keep it in place.

Go and look at the screen from a distance or even in a darkened room and light the candles on the cake. The effect is amazing.

Nursery Frieze

*T*his cake is for Jessica
Stansfeld who will be three in
December. In her nursery in the
New Forest there is a brightly
coloured frieze with the letters
of the alphabet and very simple
illustrations. This gave me the
inspiration for the cake.

The basic idea is very simple.
You use squares of sponge, cut
from a big square cake, covered
with painted fondant icing,
decorated with letters spelling
your child's name and designs
of favourite objects.

The effect comes from using
lovely bright colours and simple
shapes together to enhance
each other. I have made a list
below of easy and popular
shapes and designs, but you
can make up lots of others.

This cake will feed at least
16 adults, and many more
children. You should allow
about four hours to ice and
decorate this cake.

<u>YOU WILL NEED:</u>

CAKE 5 egg Madeira baked in a 9 to 10
inch (22.5–25 cm) square tin

ICING 1½ lb (675 gm) white fondant icing
8 oz (225 gm) white marzipan
4 oz/8 oz (110/225 gm) quantity of
butter icing (p. 14)

JAM 4–6 oz (110–175 gm) warm, sieved
apricot jam

COLOURINGS As many as you can find,
liquid or paste
Silver and gold non-toxic poster paint

DECORATIONS Smarties
Silver balls
Coloured balls
Angelica
Other small sweets

EXTRAS Long board or big square one for
cake, depending on length of name
Coloured paper or foil
Candles and holders

*You will need tweezers and a paint brush
for this cake*

The day before the party, ice the top of
the big cake, frozen or unfrozen, with
the fondant icing kneaded together and
rolled out thickly. Cut the cake into 16
equal squares and put on a big rack or
piece of Bakewell paper.

Paint the fondant squares in
different colours, trying not to slosh
the paint on too much because then it
takes so long to dry. Don't try and
make the colour too even: half the
charm is slightly patchy colour.

Cover the sides of the cake blocks with a thinnish layer of lemon butter icing, forked to give it a pretty finish. This bit is important. Otherwise the cake will dry out since you cannot cover it with clingfilm because of the wet fondant.

You can now leave the cake until the next day if you like and concentrate on your designs. You should leave it for a couple of hours to dry anyway.

If you have time and inclination, make a little plan of what colours you are going to use to make the most of the frieze. I have to say that I didn't bother and the effect was still very good – I just thought it could have been better had I taken the extra time. Cut out the letters using the stencils on page 122 and paint them. Put them on Bakewell paper to dry – this applies to all the marzipan shapes you make.

Make any of your child's favourite objects from the stencils on page 124: cat, butterfly, fish, bird, moon and stars, sun, teddy bear, balloon are all ideal.

Use small sweets to make other designs: Smarties or other small round sweets to make dice; or Smarties and angelica to make simple flowers, for example.

Use scraps of marzipan and Peanut Treets to make the bees described in the Winnie the Pooh cake (p. 63).

Use silver and coloured balls to make zig-zag or other patterns across the coloured icing.

If you were in a terrific hurry, you could use those little marzipan fruits you can buy or chocolate animals. Strawberries or other colourful real fruit would look very pretty on pastel painted fondant.

This cake looks good on very dark blue or red paper. Depending on the length of your child's name, make either a long or a diamond-shaped cake on a board the appropriate shape. A very large tray turned upside down, a plank of wood or an enormous chopping board all make good cake boards.

Assemble the cake the next day. Glue the stencils and designs to the coloured squares with a little jam. Transfer the squares with a palette knife or fish slice to the covered cake board and push them together. Don't slide them about too much, because the butter icing leaves a mark on the paper.

There really is no wrong and right with this cake – just let your imagination run riot and it will be wonderful.

Space Shuttle

This cake was fairly faithfully copied from a picture of the first Space Shuttle, Columbia, setting off on its mission on April 12th, 1981.

This cake had a lot of design difficulties in its early stages. I tried to make it vertical but that proved impossible. Then I tried using fondant icing on the shuttle and the rocket but that cracked. Then, suddenly, just as I was about to abandon it, I tried marzipan, put the board at a slope and, abracadabra, it became extremely easy and quick to do. I don't recommend making the Swiss rolls for this cake: you need the peculiar kind of synthetic firmness that only comes with bought Swiss rolls and anyway children like them – I mean really, they told me so!

In case you are wondering about the special effects in the photograph, our wonderful photographer, Chris Ridley, had us all waving sparklers, white hands swathed in black velvet!

You can make up the parts for this cake the day before, leave them overnight on Bakewell paper and assemble them the next day, a few hours before the party.

This cake is very easy, but a bit fiddly so allow three hours to complete it.

It will feed about 16 children.

YOU WILL NEED:

CAKE 2 Swiss rolls about 9 inches (22 cm) long, not iced. Freeze these before icing

ICING 1 lb (450 gm) white marzipan
Meringues made with 4 egg whites and 9 oz (255 gm) caster sugar, ¼ pt (150 ml) double cream whipped (p. 15)

JAM 6 oz (175 gm) warm, sieved apricot jam

COLOURINGS Blue paste or liquid
Silver non-toxic poster paint

DECORATIONS 2 large tubes of Smarties
2 ice cream cornets (cones)
1 box of silver balls (dragées)
1 box of coloured balls (dragées)

EXTRAS Silver foil and stiff silver card
2 × 14 inch (35 cm) square cake boards
Blue wrapping paper and silver stars
Glue, sellotape, 1½ inch (3.5 cm) screw

2 × 6 inch (15 cm) by 1¼ inch (3 cm) batons or similar
Yellow candles and silver and gold painted candle holders
The same number of Ferrero Rocher chocolate hazelnuts or large chocolates covered with gold foil

You will need tweezers and a paint brush for this cake

Make the meringues (p. 15) and while they are cooking, start icing the rocket and the shuttle. Each is made from a frozen Swiss roll, and the shuttle sits on top of the rocket. The rocket is a Swiss roll with a wedge cut from the bottom so that it rests securely on the sloping board. The wedge is about 1 inch (2.5 cm) deep, cut at an angle of about 45°.

Cut a similar wedge from the bottom of the other Swiss roll, to make the base of the shuttle. The nose cone of the shuttle is made by cutting a wedge either side of the other end to make a rounded point, and a very flat rounded wedge from that end to form the sloping pointed nose.

Lay both on Bakewell paper and brush them with jam leaving about an inch (2.5 cm) at the back.

The space shuttle is made up of four main parts:

Two side – or booster – rockets, which are tubes of Smarties covered with silver foil. Their nose cones are made of sawn off ice cream cornets, fixed with a worm of marzipan. The cornets and the marzipan are painted silver.

A shuttle, made of a Swiss roll, covered with blue marzipan and studded with silver balls. The Swiss roll is carved from the top end to form the shape of the nose cone. A wedge is cut from the other end so that it rests securely on the rocket which in turn is lying against the sloping cake board.

A rocket which supports the shuttle. The rocket is made of a Swiss roll covered with silver painted marzipan partially studded with silver and gold balls. A wedge is cut from the base so that it sits securely on the sloping cake board. A silver cardboard cone is attached to the top with a worm of silver marzipan to form the nose cone.

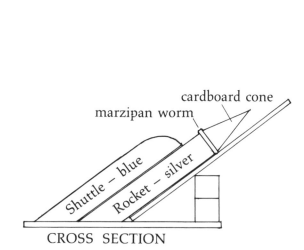

cardboard cone
marzipan worm
Shuttle – blue
Rocket – silver

CROSS SECTION

Colour one block of white marzipan bright blue. Roll it out and cover the front, sides and cone of the shuttle, tucking it under the shuttle but not covering the back. Trim the edges neatly and evenly so that the shuttle will not wobble when placed on the rocket.

Cover the rocket Swiss roll with white marzipan, leaving the same gap at the back but completely covering the top and bottom. Paint it with silver paint and leave to dry.

Keep the leftover marzipan wrapped in clingfilm.

Stud the blue shuttle with silver balls as shown in the photograph. Pick them up with tweezers, dip them in jam and push them in firmly. This process is time-consuming and there is no short cut. Then stud the rocket with silver and gold balls in a V pattern, one row silver and one gold.

Cut a semicircle of the silver card for the rocket's nose cone. The radius (depth) should be 3½ inches (9 cm). Fold the card in half along the straight side and twist it to form a cone. If necessary you can make the cone smaller by pulling the bottom edge in. Try it out to see if it fits then fix the cone securely with staples or sellotape. Put it in position on top of the rocket, pushed well on to the marzipan top,

and use a large worm of leftover marzipan, one side smeared with jam, to anchor it in position. Join the worm at the back and paint it silver.

Leave the rocket and the shuttle to dry in a cool place on Bakewell paper.

From the silver card, cut out four fins. Cut two first and then reverse the stencil so that you can stick them together and make a pair of fins. Glue them, neaten the edges and leave them to dry on Bakewell paper under a big book.

Now make the two side or booster rockets. These are tubes of Smarties with shorn-off ice cream cornets as the nose cones. Cover the tubes of Smarties with silver foil, fixed with sellotape. Smear some apricot jam on the tops and fix on small lumps of leftover marzipan, the same circumference as the tops and half an inch (1 cm) deep. Using a knife with a serrated edge, cut the cornets in half so that they have no rim. Cover with foil. Fix on to the tubes of Smarties using the lumps of marzipan to stop them falling around. Finish off by brushing a little jam on the joins and fixing on slim marzipan worms painted silver. Leave the rockets to dry upright propped in an egg holder or something similar.

The launching pad is made from two 14 inch (35 cm) square cake boards.

Cover one with silver card for the base. Make a wedge at the back by glueing two 1¼ inch (3 cm) batons of wood about 6 inches (15 cm) long together lengthways so that you have a block 2½ inches (6 cm) high and 6 inches (15 cm) long. Glue this block lengthways to the back of the base. Leave to dry. Position the bottom of the other board about 6 inches (15 cm) from that block and parallel to it. Let it rest on the block at an angle of about 40°. Fix the sloping board to the base board by putting a large screw through the middle of the base of the sloping board into the base board. Glue blue starry paper to this board. Make a crescent moon out of silver card and fix it on.

Assemble the cake two or three hours before the party. Lean the rocket against the sky and make sure it is resting securely on the base. Sit the shuttle firmly on rocket and base. Lay the little rockets on the board beside the big rocket, wedging them with small pieces of leftover marzipan at their bases. Arrange the meringues, fixing them around the shuttle with splodges of whipped cream. Make two shallow cuts down the sides of the shuttle and gently push the fins in, letting them rest on the meringues. Press the candles and holders into the Ferrero Rocher chocolates and anchor them at the front by dabbing their bases with jam.

Easter Nest

This cake was first made for Stephanie Cran's birthday which coincided with Easter. I raided the garden for spring flowers to garland the cake on its straw tray – my fruit basket! It looked lovely and very spring-like.

The basic recipe for the little marzipan eggs comes from Sara Paston Williams' charming book on Christmas and Festive Day Recipes and I have adapted her suggestions to use for this cake. This is a cake you will enjoy making even at the end of a long day. You can sit down to make most of it in front of television or listening to the radio. I made it about 10 p.m. one night near my deadline for this book and it took a leisurely hour and a half to decorate, including making all the eggs. If you hurried, you could probably do it in an hour.

It will feed about 12 people.

YOU WILL NEED:

CAKE 1 lemon sponge pudding basin cake, baked in a basin bigger than 2 pints (1.1 litre). Use a 3 or 4 egg mixture, and if you use a 4 egg mixture, the basin should be over 3 pints (1.7 litres)

ICING Lemon butter icing, 4 oz/8 oz (110/225 gm) mixture for the 3 egg cake, 6 oz/12 oz (175/335 gm) for the 4 egg (p. 14)

COLOURINGS Pastel colours: green, blue, violet, pink, yellow, for the eggs

DECORATIONS 1 box of chocolate Matchmakers, orange flavoured
1 small box of angelica (1 oz/30 gm size)
Crystallised roses, violets, mimosa and coloured sugar balls – any of these or similar
Real spring flowers, – daffodils, violets, primroses, cowslips, appleblossom (or fabric flowers)

MARZIPAN EGGS 8 oz (225 gm) white marzipan
2 oz (55 gm) caster sugar

EXTRAS 1 egg
Cocktail sticks
Flat basket or straw tray

Put the cake (frozen or unfrozen) on an upturned pudding basin.

Make the butter icing with butter, icing sugar and lemon juice. Cover the cake with it using a small table or palette knife. It should be fairly thick and a bit roughed up.

Leave the cake on one side while you make the eggs.

Divide the marzipan into as many portions as you have pastel colours. Do not mix in the colours evenly – mottled and speckly colouring adds to the eggs' appearance.

Dye the sugar, also divided into three or four, by putting a spot of colour into the middle of each pile and mixing it around with the back of a teaspoon until all the sugar grains are coloured – again this doesn't have to be even. I made about 16 to 20 eggs out of ½ lb (225 gm) of marzipan using a big teaspoon dug in and round the lump of marzipan to get the approximate size.

Roll the little lumps of marzipan round in your palms to smooth them out. Then gently pull them into egg shapes, a bit pointed at one end.

Froth up the white of an egg, skewer each egg with a cocktail stick and dip it first into the egg white and then into the coloured sugars. Put on a cake rack, grill pan or piece of Bakewell paper to dry.

Now back to the nest. Snap each Matchmaker in halves or thirds, and push them into the sides of the cake in a criss cross way, like twigs on a nest. Now cut up the angelica into pieces about ⅔ inch (2 cm) long and quite thin, and stick them in too.

Use the cake decorations to decorate the nest as you wish. The basic rule is the more the merrier.

When the colour on the eggs is dry, pile them up on the top. Put a disc of Bakewell paper or a small plate under the cake and lay it on a straw tray or basket. Lift the cake with a fish slice. Leave it in a cool place overnight. Next day, press in small fresh or fabric flowers round the nest and surround it with blossom or larger flowers.

I 'borrowed' the ducklings from the Ark to set in front of the Easter nest because they looked right there, rather like spring chicks. The instructions for making them are on p. 85

Hallowe'en Witch

I find this demented-looking witch very engaging. There are a lot of rather serious and sinister witches zooming around on their broomsticks for Hallowe'en and I fancied making a jolly one. She is dressed up in her best for this Annual Outing, but it doesn't look as if she will ever manage to get her very solid broomstick off the pumpkin launching pad, although she is grimly determined to try.

Oasis — that solid green foam used by florists — makes a firm base for the candles. It is inflammable, so put out the candles before they burn down to the bases.

You will get 24 or more rather odd-shaped slices from this cake. It will take you about an hour and a half to decorate.

Be careful of the cocktail sticks when children are eating this cake.

YOU WILL NEED:

CAKES 2 pudding basin cakes each made from a 3 egg Victoria sponge mixture. Make them in big wide pudding basins (3 to 4 pints, or 1.5 to 2 litres)

ICING 1½ lb (675 gm) yellow marzipan to cover the pumpkin
8 oz (225 gm) white marzipan to make the witch and the cat.

JAM 6 oz (175 gm) warm, sieved apricot jam

DECORATIONS 1 Cadbury's Flake
1 box Chocolate Matchmakers
1 liquorice pinwheel or small circle of card
1 pointed ice cream cornet or more card
1 glacé cherry
Shredded coconut
Coloured balls (dragées)

COLOURINGS Orange, yellow, green liquid or paste
Black and purple paste
Silver colouring powder or non-toxic colouring paint

EXTRAS Cocktail sticks
14 inch (35 cm) round cake board
Black or purple paper
8 tall dark blue or purple or black candles
1 brick of Oasis cut into 8 pieces and covered with foil for candle holders
Coloured merit stars

You will need tweezers and glue for this cake

Take the two pudding basin cakes, frozen or unfrozen, level the tops and glue these flat sides together with apricot jam, to make the pumpkin.

Cover the whole cake with jam.

Dye the 1½ lb (675 gm) of yellow marzipan with orange colouring. If you have white marzipan, put some yellow colouring in with the orange and mix it all together leaving the marzipan a bit blotchy – the pumpkin looks more real that way.

With a small sharp knife, divide the cake into six sections running downwards like an orange. You only need to make a little notch to indicate the line. Put about 1 oz (30 gm) marzipan aside for the broomstick. Divide the rest into six portions. Roll out the marzipan between your palms so that each portion is like a torpedo, pointed at each end, fat in the middle, and as long as the depth of the cake from top centre to the board – probably about 7 inches (17 cm). Now mould a marzipan portion on to each section of the cake, pushing it out to the edges of the section and into the shallow groove.

When you have finished the six sections, you may feel that the surface of the pumpkin is a bit too rough. If so, cover a jam jar with clingfilm and roll it over the surface of the cake to smooth it. With a skewer, make grooves in the icing between each initial groove so that the pumpkin has twelve sections.

Now make the broomstick. Colour the leftover piece of marzipan from the cake brown. Take the Cadbury's Flake and brush jam over the end. Cut up four or five long Matchmakers, or use about sixteen short ones, and push these into the marzipan. You have to push them in parallel to the flake; if you try to make them stick out, they fall off. Leave the broomstick on one side to dry with the tail propped up.

It's time for the inscrutable cat, who is made of 2½ oz (70 gm) of black marzipan. Dye the marzipan with paste if you can, or it will be very soft. Use just over ½ oz (15 gm) for the head, making a ball, and then pulling out the ears. Make a worm for the tail, about 2½ inches (6 cm) long and ⅓ inch (1 cm) fat. Make a big ball for the body out of the rest of the marzipan and fix the head and tail on with apricot jam. Using tweezers, push in two green balls for eyes, one pink ball for a nose and short pieces of shredded coconut as whiskers. Leave the cat to dry on a sheet of Bakewell paper.

Cover the round cake board with a circle of black or purple paper and make the Oasis candle holders.

Lastly the witch. Dye some shredded coconut bright green and leave on one side. Start off with her hat. This is the top of an ice cream cone. Cut it just

above the rim with a small serrated knife. Cover the cone with silver foil and stick on the coloured merit stars. Stuff a small ball of marzipan, any colour, into the cone.

Make the base out of a liquorice pinwheel, if you have one, or a circle of silver card painted silver on the underside too. Push a cocktail stick through the base of the cone and up through the marzipan, pushing enough out the other end to go through the head.

Take another ounce (30 gm) of marzipan, dyed yellow, for her head, hands and feet. Make a ball for her head, paint part of it with jam and push in the strands of green shredded coconut using tweezers. Push in two pink balls for eyes and pull out a bit of yellow marzipan for her nose. Either paint on a big red mouth or use a piece of glacé cherry. Put on one side to set. Make four round yellow balls for her feet and hands and set aside.

Use the rest of the marzipan – there should be about 4 oz (110 gm) – for the body. Dye it all a good deep purple. Take a scrap and roll it into a narrow band to go round her hat. Anchor it with apricot jam. Take 3 oz (85 gm) and roll it into a big ball for her body and put on one side on Bakewell paper. With the remaining purple marzipan,

make four thinnish worms and wind them round the middles of 4 short Matchmakers or 2 long ones halved. Push a ball of yellow marzipan on to one end of each Matchmaker. On two of these fix silver balls in the shape of a buckle to look like her Hallowe'en best shoes. Using a cocktail stick, attach the witch's head to her body. Now push the Matchmakers into the body as arms and legs at the most acute angle you can – she should look as if she is playing hockey.

Put the broomstick on the top of the cake and push it well down. Put the witch on top and make certain she is secure. You can push the body down and round the flake so that it hugs it tightly. Now put the hat on top. Do this last because it is quite heavy and to get it balanced, you need to have the whole witch in position on the pumpkin. Now use tweezers to dip pink balls in jam and stick them on her chest in a W shape.

Put the cat on the top of the pumpkin by the end of the broomstick.

You can happily leave this cake overnight in a cool dry place. Just before, push the long candles into their holders and light them. The candles in the photograph were cut to different lengths to 'frame' the cake. It looks very ghostly but still quite jolly.

Guy Fawkes

My first memory of a decorated party cake is one made by my mother for November 5th when my brother and I were little. I remember that the guy was dressed in bright colours and that his hat was made of green marzipan. I also remember that his arms had to be propped up with cocktail sticks because they kept falling off!

The bonfire is a pudding basin cake covered with chocolate butter icing and studded with Matchmaker twigs. If you have a very mild day and can take the cake and the children outside, you can use a Catherine wheel to produce the magical effect in the photograph. But be sure to keep everyone a safe distance from the fireworks.

Be careful of the cocktail sticks when children start attacking the cake.

This cake should not take you more than one and a half hours to decorate and it will feed about 12 people.

YOU WILL NEED:

CAKE Chocolate pudding basin sponge, made with a 3 egg mixture in a basin at least 2 pints (1.1. litres) capacity

ICING Chocolate butter icing made with 4 oz/8 oz (110/225 gm) mixture and 3 oz (85 gm) chocolate powder melted in 1 tbsp coffee (page 14)
8 oz (225 gm) white fondant icing
8 oz (225 gm) white marzipan

JAM 4 oz (110 gm) warm, sieved apricot jam

COLOURINGS Green, pink, yellow, orange, bright blue, red, purple, brown

DECORATIONS 1 box long or short Matchmakers
2 packets Mini Flakes or 8 large Chocolate Flakes cut up
1 small packet of Chocolate Flock – flaked plain chocolate
4 Chocolate Polka Dots or raisins

EXTRAS 14 inch (35 cm) round cake board
Green wrapping or art paper
Yellow candles and holders
Cocktail sticks

Make the guy first.

The body is marzipan and his clothes are coloured fondant. Make his head out of 1 oz (30 gm) marzipan and paint it pink with brown eyes and moustache. Put on one side, on a sheet of Bakewell paper.

Form his body out of 3 oz (85 gm)

of marzipan in a rectangular block slightly broader at the shoulders and narrower at the waist, about 2 inches (5 cm) tall and wide and 1 inch (2.5 cm) from back to front. Make 2 fat sausages for arms weighing ½ oz (15 gm) each and fix them to his shoulders with cocktail sticks.

Take the remaining 3 oz (85 gm) and divide it into 2 for his legs and feet. Form them into fat sausages and pull the knees up and the feet out. Put on one side on Bakewell paper.

Brush all the bits of marzipan with a little jam.

Now for his clothes and make-up.

Colour a scant ounce (30 gm) of fondant yellow and put it on to his head like a wig. Paint on a few strands of orange. Take another ounce (30 gm) and pull it into a thick circle about 2 inches (5 cm) round and then pull up the bit in the middle for the crown of the hat. Put it on his head and then make the brim turn up and down in a realistic way. Paint it bright green.

Roll out a 2 oz (55 gm) lump of bright red fondant thinly into a circle. Put this over his body and arms. Push together under his arms and at his sides and neaten off.

Fix his head into his body with a cocktail stick. Colour 3 oz (85 gm) of fondant bright blue. Roll it out thinly and use a triangle about 2 × 1 inch (5 × 2.5 cm) for his kerchief. Turn up the edges and fold it a bit as you put it on.

Cover his legs, except for his feet, with the rest of the blue fondant, laying it over the fronts and joining at the back.

Stick four Polka Dots in to the front of his jacket for big buttons.

I coloured his gloves and boots a rather strange purple but they might be better brown or black. They are made out of the remaining ounce (30 gm) of fondant, divided into four lumps rolled out thinly into circles about 1½ inches (3.5 cm) in diameter. Stick these over his white marzipan hands and feet.

Spread the chocolate butter icing all over the bonfire and stick in the Matchmakers. Arrange the guy on top of the fire by pushing his torso into the icing and then arranging his legs next to it. Put the candles all round. Keep the cake in a cool place until the party. Then lift it with a large fish slice on to the cake board, covered with green paper.

Strew flaked chocolate on the green paper, and then put the small Chocolate Flakes all round the base of the fire to look like logs.

Christmas Tree

It is very hard to come up with a new idea for a Christmas cake, but this one is easy, fun and suitable for both children and grown ups because it is a combination of both sponge and fruit cakes. This is one time when it is important to use Madeira (made by hand or mixer, <u>not</u> food processor) for the tree if you want it to stand up. Madeira is much firmer than Victoria sponge, so when you cut a slot in the fruit cake base and wedge the Madeira cake firmly into it, the tree should stay upright with no trouble.

I made this cake for Katie and Georgina Campbell, aged 8 and 5, who are my nearly next door neighbours.

It is wiser not to put the candles in until party time. The candleholder pins tend to crack the sponge and you may lose a branch or see it wobbling precariously.

You should begin decorating this cake at least one day before you want to eat it because the Royal icing must have time to set lying down before you stand it upright. If it is not set, it slides lugubriously to the bottom of the tree and collects in a flurry there. The cake keeps well so you could make it a few days in advance and assemble it on the day. I bought the cake base but you can make it if you wish.

<u>YOU WILL NEED:</u>

CAKE 8 inch (20 cm) square frozen Madeira made with 4 egg mixture 6 inch (15 cm) round fruit cake (bought or made with 2 egg mixture)

ICING 8 oz (225 gm) marzipan to cover fruit cake 8 oz (225 gm) red fondant to cover fruit cake 1 lb (450 gm) green marzipan to cover sponge cake 8 oz (225 gm) Royal icing to cover front of sponge cake.

JAM 6–8 oz (175–225 gm) warm, sieved apricot jam

COLOURINGS Red and green, paste or liquid

DECORATIONS Coloured balls (dragées)

CHRISTMAS TREE

Chocolate vermicelli or flock
Tiny boxes of sweets wrapped as presents
Small coloured sweets
Glacé cherries

EXTRAS 14 inch (35 cm) round or square
cake board covered with dark green shiny paper
Icing sugar to go on board like snow
Coloured Christmas candles and holders
A decoration for the top of the tree or
silver or gold card to make a star (I used
a peacock kindly supplied by Graham
and Green)

You will need tweezers for this cake

Cover the fruit cake with marzipan,
using a circle for the top and a strip
for the sides.
   Then cut out the tree from the
Madeira, using the stencil.
Lay the straight
side of the stencil on a
diagonal of the
cake and cut out
the right hand side;
reverse the stencil and,
still with the straight side
down the diagonal, cut the
left hand side to match. You
will find it easy to do if the
Madeira is frozen, or at least chilled.
   Now put the base of the Madeira
cake on top of the fruit cake and draw a
line round the bottom so that you can
cut out the slot for the base of the tree
to fit in. Cut out the slot in the fruit

Centre line

BASE SLOT DO NOT ICE

cake, digging down about ½ inch (1 cm).

Brush the sponge cake with the warm jam, except for the base which will slot into the fruit cake. Roll out the green marzipan and cut out two tree shapes with the stencil for the front and back of the tree. Follow the stencil exactly but omit the base – do not cover this part of the tree with icing – marzipan or Royal. Roll out the remainder again and cut into strips 2 inches (5 cm) wide to fit the sides of the tree. Take the slightly rounded top of the Madeira as the front and cover this with the tree-shaped marzipan. Turn it over on to Bakewell paper and cover the back. Now stand it upright and tuck the strips of marzipan down the sides: something like a knitting needle or rounded skewer is helpful for pushing the marzipan up and under the branches. Lie the cake on its back and leave the marzipan to dry a little whilst you make the Royal icing. Follow the recipe on page 14 but do not add any glycerine, which makes it too soft for this cake.

Brush a very thin layer of jam over the green marzipan front of the tree cake and then put the Royal icing on, using a knife. Rough it up a little as you go.

Whilst the icing is soft, decorate it with festoons of coloured balls. Using tweezers, dip these in a saucer of warm jam and then push them firmly into the icing. Fix on other small sweets and glacé cherries with jam.

When you have finished, put the cake on a piece of Bakewell paper in a cool airy place. Leave at least overnight to set.

Next turn the fruit cake upside down, brush a thin film of jam over it and cover it all with the red fondant. It should look like an upside down red flowerpot. Trim it neatly at the edge and use the trimmings to make a red fondant worm for a rim. Fix on with jam and leave the cake on one side.

Cover the board with dark green paper – or whatever colour you like – and make the presents to go under the tree the next day. Also make the star to go on the top. Assemble the cake near the time of the party. Turn the fruit cake the right way up, put it on the board with the presents around it. Brush the top with jam and put chocolate vermicelli on it to look like earth. Pick up the tree cake, which should be pretty hard by now and drop it in the slot. Push it down carefully but firmly.

Put the star or other decoration at the top in a little cut and then put the candles at the ends of the branches. Light the candles at teatime – and you have a real Christmas Tree cake.

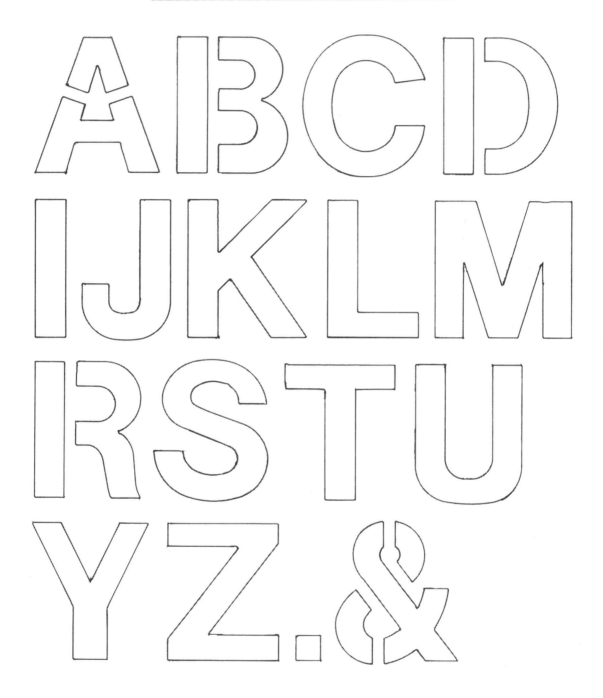

N.B. IF YOU PREFER LETTERS AND NUMBERS
WITHOUT GAPS JUST JOIN UP THE OUTLINES
AND THEN TRACE.

BASIC STENCILS

LETTERING

Piping

It is possible that some of you will feel compelled to pipe – names, dates, Happy Birthday etc. Piping is not difficult – really – but it does unfortunately need practice. However, this book is not about being perfect and as you can see from my wobbly name on the cover, even imperfect piping looks fun.

Books about icing wedding cakes and grand things like that tell you on no account to use glacé icing. I strongly suggest you use it because it is so quick to make and produces perfectly acceptable if not immaculate results.

The quantities below are very rough – I always put in too much water and then have to stiffen it up again with some more icing sugar, so look on these as guidelines only:

4 oz (110 gm) sieved icing sugar
1 tbsp warm water
Few drops of colouring

The consistency is the most important thing in successful piping and it is almost impossible to describe. I can only say that glacé icing should be stiff enough to curl round when you trail the spoon in it and make some attempt to hold a peak but that it shouldn't actually manage it.

I have never got into nozzles – I use one thin one for writing and that is all. It comes with the icing set which I bought in the local hardware store and looks like a syringe.

Do not attempt to ice on a wet surface because the piping will sink in and get lost. If this happens turn to Disasters (p. 128) for rescue operations.

Ice on a dry surface and hold the syringe almost vertically above the spot you wish to write on. It helps to practise on a piece of paper first, in case the icing is too runny.

Stencil letters

On page 122, you will find stencils for the alphabet in capital letters. Trace these letters on to Bakewell paper, put them on rolled out marzipan and cut round them with a small sharp knife with the blade dipped in hot water and shaken dry. If the blade is too wet, the marzipan becomes gooey.

Don't try and lift these letters on to the cake as they are. Put them on a sheet of Bakewell paper in the freezer or fridge for half an hour. You will then be able to lift them easily and peel the paper off before putting them on the cake.

You can colour the marzipan before making the letters or paint the letters afterwards.

Writing in fondant and marzipan

This is very easy and the results are good. Take a small piece of either fondant icing or marzipan, say about ½ oz (15 gm), knead it and then pull it into a fat sausage. Put a piece of Bakewell paper on a board and roll the sausage back and forth with your finger tips until it stretches into a long thin worm. You will find you can make it fairly even if you move the action from side to side a little.

Check the area you have on the cake for writing and gauge the size of your lettering accordingly.

Now form a letter at a time and cut the pieces off with your thumbnail – or a knife. When you get good at this, try joined up writing, using the long worms to make letters running into each other.

You can use coloured marzipan to make letters but do not try to colour fondant before rolling the letters: it will be too soft. Paint it afterwards if you want to.

I am usually in a hurry to finish the cake so I put the lettering on straight away, as long as the surface of the cake is not wet. If you have time, however, leave the letters on Bakewell paper until they are dry and firm, or put them in the freezer to set quickly.

BITS AND PIECES

Cake Boards

These are standard stock at most stationery or big department stores. You can easily improvise your own base from chipboard or cardboard, a tray or pastry board.

A simple cake becomes exciting and impressive with a well chosen background. Wrapping paper, art paper and remnants of material are all useful.

You can also use small sweets and decorations, such as Cadbury's Buttons, popcorn, or hundreds and thousands (see the Marshmallow Garden, page 35).

Sticky Stuff

Ordinary glue, spray glue or sticky tape sticks paper neatly to a cake board. Sticky tape, a staple gun or drawing pins fix material most easily. Use apricot jam to fix edible backgrounds on to the cake board.

Covering Cake Boards with Paper

1. Square: Apply glue to surface. Leave a few minutes to get tacky. Put covering paper on board and leave to set for 10–20 minutes. Trim paper, leaving 2–3 inches (5–7.5cm) all round. Apply glue to flaps of paper, leave to get tacky. Neatly fold paper on to back of board, trimming any excess paper as you go.
2. Round: Cover top and not sides. Put board down on wrong side of paper and trace round outline with a pencil. These boards are seldom exactly round, so make corresponding pairs of pencil marks at two points on board and paper so that you can match them.

Cake Decorations

I have used sweets, candles and other small decorations which are easily available everywhere. However if you cannot get hold of the particular kind I have used, don't worry – just substitute something similar. Ordinary candle holders can be made more glamorous if you paint them with a couple of coats of gold or silver poster paint. For real impact, push the candles and holders into big foil wrapped chocolates.

DISASTERS

Dry Sponge Cake

If you are worried that your cake is dry, one way to make it seem more moist is to split it and fill it with a very gooey butter icing. If it is a lemon cake, use lemon curd.

Holes Large and Small

When I first started on this new cake-making career, my cakes were regularly pitted and pockmarked and worst of all sometimes had big holes in the middle.

I didn't know then what I know now about curdling (see page 8) and thought these holes were an occupational hazard for cake cooks.

So, from necessity, I evolved ways of dealing with the problem, filling the holes and craters with butter icing which behaves like a Polyfilla for cakes.

Big cakes sometimes crack and you can use the same methods to salvage these.

It is important for you to realise that the cakes will be delicious. I used to save my disasters for dinner parties when grown-ups went into a state of ecstasy about gaping holes in the middle of gooey cakes. Almost everything can be disguised and will be fine, provided it tastes good.

When the holey cake is completely cool, inspect the damage and then put it carefully in the freezer. If there is a big dip in the middle, make a good quantity of stiff butter icing – don't put any liquid in it. I make a mixture of about 4 oz (110 gm) butter and 8 oz (225 gm) icing sugar for rescue purposes.

When the cake is chilled, or preferably frozen, use the butter icing and a palette knife to patch up all the cracks and sandwich it together. Put it back in the freezer to set firm.

This cake will now be perfectly suitable for decorating as a whole cake. But do be careful of the cake – don't try to cut up before decorating and consider the nature of the cake you intend to make. I made the prototype Easter Nest Cake (p. 109) from a pudding basin cake which had recently been in four pieces. The cake was fine in a cool place, well glued with butter icing, but about 8 o'clock that night, there was a minor explosion as the nest fell apart and all the eggs went skidding over the floor.

Keep your Polyfilla'd cake in the fridge until an hour or two before the party to be on the safe side.

No icing for the corners of the cake

Your best bet for this is candles, or rather candleholders. The Guardsman (p. 87) was a case in point. The icing just would not stretch to the corners so I had to patch them. Even though I put lots of dredging mixture on the joins, they still showed. So I made candleholders from scraps of red marzipan, put silver balls round them and blue candles in them. The design of the cake was much better – and no cracks showed.

Not enough fondant or marzipan

If you realise with horror that you don't have enough icing, fondant or marzipan, to cover the sides of a cake as well as the top, don't worry. Trim the icing to fit the top. Make some flavoured butter icing, a 4 oz/8 oz (110 gm/225 gm) mixture is a good start, and use it to cover the sides.

Make a ribbed pattern with a fork or spread it smooth with a palette knife. It is usually best to leave the butter icing its natural creamy colour but you could colour it if you wanted to. Sometimes it looks even better than before and it always tastes delicious.

Fondant is too soft when coloured

This was my most frequent problem with fondant icing at the beginning. In order to get a nice deep colour, I added so much cake colouring liquid that the fondant was too runny to roll out. This also happened to marzipan but not quite so easily.

Either only use cake colouring paste available from specialist cook shops to produce bright or deep colours or paint the cakes after you have put on the icing.

If you have already coloured the icing and it is running around, knead in enough icing sugar to make it stiff, try rolling it out between sheets of Bakewell or greaseproof paper, and if the colour is too pale, paint it after you put it on the cake.

Cracks in fondant

Fondant icing sometimes seems to crack for no reason at all and it is almost certainly not your fault.

If the icing is not painted, rub it with dredging mixture (half icing sugar and half cornflour). Use your forefinger and go on rubbing until the crack is so faint you can scarcely see it.

If the cake is painted, put a candle or some other decoration over the top – it's the only way.

Alternatively, don't worry about doing anything, you are probably the only person who will notice.

(Marzipan never seems to crack so there is no note about it.)

Putting fondant or marzipan in the wrong place

I used to aim completely wrong and position a large piece of icing with one half draping over the plate I was icing on and the other half trying to cover the cake.

If you are quick and deft, you can usually catch up the icing on your rolling pin and re-position it.

If you cannot do this, you are left with a jammy piece of icing. Lift it up and carefully sponge off the jam and crumbs with a slightly wet cloth. This is easier with marzipan but also works with fondant. Then pick up the icing and knead it all together. Start again.

Sinking piping

This is usually caused by icing on a wet surface or using icing that is too runny. Let it dry completely and then re-pipe over the top, using the sunken icing as a base. It will look rather good. If you re-ice in a slightly different shade, or even a different colour, it will look as if you meant the whole thing anyway.

You put a cake with coloured decorations on it in the freezer and the colours run as the cake thaws

This happened to the Computer cake (p. 96). I decorated it with Smarties, put it in the freezer, took it out to be photographed and the colours ran all down the front. What a disaster – everyone was watching, too, which made it worse. The solution is to remove the Smarties, wash the fondant with a soft brush dipped in water until the icing is completely clean and then substitute different sweets such as jellies and gums (brushed with jam) so that it doesn't happen again. You can then put it back in the freezer briefly to make sure that the substitute decorations stay in place.